Mixed Martial Arts

Analyses of Techniques & Usage

An
Anthology
of Articles
from the
*Journal of
Asian Martial Arts*
Edited by Michael A. DeMarco, M.A.

Disclaimer
Please note that the authors and publisher of this book are not responsible in any manner whatsoever for any injury that may result from practicing the techniques and/or following the instructions given within. Since the physical activities described herein may be too strenuous in nature for some readers to engage in safely, it is essential that a physician be consulted prior to training.

All Rights Reserved
No part of this publication, including illustrations, may be reproduced or utilized in any form or by any means, electronic or mechanical, including photocopying, recording, or by any information storage and retrieval system (beyond that copying permitted by sections 107 and 108 of the US Copyright Law and except by reviewers for the public press), without written permission from Via Media Publishing Company.

Warning: Any unauthorized act in relation to a copyright work may result in both a civil claim for damages and criminal prosecution.

Copyright © 2015 by
Via Media Publishing Company
941 Calle Mejia #822
Santa Fe, NM 87501 USA
E-mail: md@goviamedia.com

All articles in this anthology were originally published in the *Journal of Asian Martial Arts*.
Listed according to the table of contents for this anthology:

Bolelli, D. (2003)	Volume 12, Number 3	pages 40–51
Bolelli, D. (2005)	Volume 14, Number 1	pages 40–51
Zerling, A. (2005)	Volume 14, Number 2	pages 80–89
Zerling, A. (2005)	Volume 14, Number 3	pages 54–63
Zerling, A. (2005)	Volume 14, Number 4	pages 74–83
Scott, S. (2007)	Volume 16, Number 3	pages 64–77
Ferguson, R. (2011)	Volume 20, Number 2	pages 74–81
Ferguson, R. (2011)	Volume 20, Number 4	pages 26–35

Book and cover design by Via Media Publishing Company
Edited by Michael A. DeMarco, M.A.
Cover illustration courtesy of www.dreamstime.com

ISBN: 978-1-893765-19-1

www.viamediapublishing.com

contents

v   **Preface**
Michael DeMarco, M.A.

viii   **Author Bio Notes**

CHAPTERS

1   Mixed Martial Arts: A Technical Analysis of the Ultimate Fighting Championship in Its Formative Years
by Daniele Bolelli, M.A.

19   Varied Approaches to Grappling in Mixed Martial Arts Competition
by Daniele Bolelli, M.A.

35   The Choke: The Ultimate Finishing Technique
by Andrew Zerling, B.S.

47   The Arm Lock: The Technique of Control
by Andrew Zerling, B.S.

57   The Leg Lock: Technique of Contrast
by Andrew Zerling, B.S.

68   Core Skills and Four Primary Applications of the Cross-Body Armlock
by Steve Scott, B.A.

85   A Study of Armbar Submissions in Ultimate Fighting Championship Contests from 2000 to 2011
by Rhadi Ferguson, Ph.D.

92   A Study of Chokehold Submissions in Ultimate Fighting Championships from 2000 to 2011
by Rhadi Ferguson, Ph.D.

100   **Index**

preface

In retrospect, all martial arts are mixed, but MMA has taken on a mystique of its own in the newest wave of combative experimentation. This book presents an encompassing perspective of this phenomenon in eight chapters written by experts in the field. In their individual chapters they provide analyses of the techniques utilized during many of the leading competitive events, mainly the Ultimate Fighting Championships (UFC), and give practical "how to" instruction.

This book pulls together some of the best writings published in the *Journal of Asian Martial Arts* regarding modern mixed martial arts. Daniele Bolelli uses a scholarly approach to produce two excellent chapters, as does Rhadi Ferguson with his two chapters. Bolelli provides a superb overview by analyzing 176 matches that took place between 1993 and 1999 under the UFC umbrella. He also highlights the different ways in which grappling techniques are currently used in mixed martial arts competition.

While utilizing a comprehensive approach, Dr. Ferguson zeros in on armbar and chokehold submissions to conclude just how often these were utilized in 1,263 UFC bouts. His works here can assist mixed martial arts professionals with analytical information to help them in training practices and winning strategies.

What do the analyses show? Well, one thing is that all the techniques used are found in many old martial traditions. Some techniques are extremely old. Certainly cavemen used chokes. Many are from the previous millennium, as hinted by the numerous Japanese terms used since the samurai sipped sake. Fundamental techniques are discussed by Andew Zerling and Steve Scott.

Four other chapters provide insightful text and the photographic detail to present the theory and practice of the major techniques utilized by mixed martial artists: chokes, armlocks, and leg locks. Zerling offers three chapters with the precious help of his teacher, Renzo Gracie. Scott's chapter is a highly detailed piece on the cross-body armlock, giving four primary applications all will appreciate as vital to MMA practice.

The eight chapters are filled with analytical text helpful for the pursuit of combat expertise. There is enough here to find of great value. But there is more. In the chapters you'll also find perspective and insight that illuminate what is occurring in the evolution of MMA competition. Read closely and you'll see that—beneath the hype—changing competitive rules and dollar amounts play a role in the outcome of championship belts and competitive crowns. We need to factor these aspects into our quest to understand the rich variety of martial traditions.

Michael A. DeMarco
Santa Fe, New Mexico
October 2015

author bio notes

Daniele Bolelli, M.A., holds a 4th-degree ranking in Kung Fu San Soo, and is a practitioner of mixed martial arts. He has an M.A. degree in American Indian studies from the University of California–Los Angeles (UCLA) and is a lecturer at UCLA, Califormia State University–Long Beach, and Santa Monica College. He is the author of *On the Warrior's Path: Philosophy, Fighting, and Martial Arts Mythology* (Frog, Ltd. 2003).

Michael A. DeMarco, M.A., received his degree from Seton Hall University's Asian Studies Department. In 1964 he began studies of Chinese–Indonesian kuntao-silat in the Willem Reeders tradition, primarily under Art Sikes, Thomas Pepperman, and Richard Lopez. Since 1973 he has focused on taijiquan: Yang style, Xiong Yanghe lineage; Chen style, Du Yuze lineage. He founded Via Media Publishing Company in 1991, producing the *Journal of Asian Martial Arts* and books. He teaches in Santa Fe, New Mexico.

Rhadi Ferguson, Ph.D., is a 2004 United States Olympian in judo, professional MMA fighter, and researcher. His current research interests include mixed martial arts and the professional development of coaching and teaching practices in combat sports. Dr. Ferguson completed his doctorate in philosophy in education from Capella University in 2009.

Steve Scott, MBA., started judo in 1965 at age of twelve and his life has been linked with judo, sambo, and jujutsu ever since. He is a 7th-degree in Kodokan Judo and 7th-degree in Shingitai Jujitsu and is a member of the Sombo Association's Hall of Fame. He graduated with a major in sociology and a minor in physical education from the University of Missouri, Kansas City.

Andrew Zerling, B.S., earned his degree in biology (with a specialization in mammalian anatomy and physiology) from Temple University in Philadelphia. Zerling has been a science writer for the food and drug industry for many years. Zerling is also an East Coast-based freelance writer and martial artist with over fifteen years training in Renzo Gracie jujutsu, judo, wrestling, and aikido.

NOTES:

Mixed Martial Arts:
A Technical Analysis of the Ultimate Fighting Championship in Its Formative Years

by Daniele Bolelli, M.A.

Attempting a flying armbar (Bob Cook vs. Tiki Ghosen).
All photos courtesy of the Ultimate Fighting Championships.

Introduction

In the modern history of martial arts, the 1990's will be remembered as the decade of the revolution. The revolution we are referring to is the advent on the martial arts scene of a new brand of combat sport that captured much popular attention and altered the training methods, philosophies, and outlooks of thousands of martial artists around the globe. Many names have been used to baptize this new combat sport—Valetudo, Ultimate Fighting, No Holds Barred Fighting, Shootfighting, etc.—but the most appropriate is perhaps mixed martial arts, since these competitions were designed to test the strengths and weaknesses of different styles under a set of very permissive rules that did not favor any particular art.

Videogames and movies had played with the idea of tournaments open to all styles of martial arts for a while. In Brazil, Valetudo competitions had been taking place for a good part of the twentieth century. In ancient Greece, Pankration, an ancestor of mixed martial arts that allowed kickboxing, throws, groundfighting and submissions (i.e. chokes and leverages), used to be a main event of the Olympic Games (Poliakoff, 1987; Vale, 2001). But in recent history, in the Western world, this form of competition was a complete novelty. Until the 1990's, in fact, the different styles of martial arts organized tournaments with such restrictive rules that made the confrontation of different arts on an even ground virtually impossible. This state of things, however, was about to change when in 1993 the first Ultimate Fighting Championship (UFC) was held in the US. Soon thereafter, the number of organizations promoting similar tournaments grew exponentially —Shooto, Rings, Pride, World Extreme Fighting, Extreme Fighting, Pancrase (actually the Japanese Pancrase predated UFC by a couple of months), King of the Cage, Absolute Fighting Championship, etc. The days of Pankration were indeed back (Bolelli, 2003).

The implications of this revolution are so many—on a moral and philosophical as well as a technical level—that entire volumes could be written on the topic. For the sake of brevity, this chapter will focus exclusively on one aspect: the technical evolution of mixed martial arts during its formative years. To be more precise, I will analyze a sample of 176 matches that took place between November 12, 1993 and September 24, 1999 under the UFC umbrella.[1] This sample covers UFC events I through XXII. The categories include the size and age of the fighters, the length of the matches, and the techniques used to win the matches. By providing detailed statistics, this essay will create a concrete basis for any further discussion of this popular, albeit misunderstood, topic.

Rules

What set the Ultimate Fighting Championship (and its imitators) apart from other kinds of martial arts competitions were its rules, so it is imperative to consider what was so unique about these rules. At first, the rules were extremely simple: there were hardly any. Two fighters from any discipline (including Western styles of wrestling, boxing, and Brazilian jujutsu, as well as many traditional Asian martial arts) would meet in an octagon surrounded by a steel cage and could use virtually any kind of martial art techniques to defeat the opponent. The only explicit prohibitions were against biting, eye gouging, and fish hooking. This was in drastic opposition to most martial arts tournaments, which allowed only a very limited range of techniques and, therefore, gave a tremendous advantage to the practitioners of those arts that focused almost exclusively on such techniques.

Submissions were used to end 67 matches (38.1%) whereas strikes were used in 72 matches (41%). Only one throw successfully ended a match (the throw has been included with the standing techniques).

To further break down the techniques, we can now analyze them separately under the following categories:

1) ground submissions,
2) ground strikes,
3) standing submissions,
4) standing strikes,
5) throws.

Genki Sudo applying a rear naked choke to Liegh Remedios. This technique stops the blood flow to the brain and causes the opponent to tap or lose consciousness.

The division between some of these categories is not as clear-cut as it may sound. In a few cases, which technique ended a match may be open to interpretation. For example, many people tend to classify Frank Shamrock's victory over Tito Ortiz in UFC XXII as the result of strikes executed by a standing Shamrock against a downed Ortiz. I file that victory as a ground submission. A few seconds before the end of the match, in fact, Shamrock had Ortiz in a guillotine choke on the ground. Although Ortiz did not tap out as a result of the choke, he did not have any energy or oxygen left to do anything once Shamrock stood up. The slaps on the head executed by Shamrock at that point were not what won the match. With this warning in mind, let us turn to the statistics.

A textbook example of an armbar (*jujigatame*) executed by Brazilian jujutsu specialist Murilo Bustamante.

A triangle choke from the guard (Ivan Salaverry vs. Andrei Semenov).

Most matches (63, which is 35.8% of the 176 matches considered) ended because of a submission applied while on the ground. This came as a surprise to most viewers who, because of some stereotypical ideas regarding how martial arts are supposed to look, expected standing kicks and punches to take the lion's share.

Out of these submissions, 41 were either chokes or neck cranks (23.3% of all matches and 65% of all ground submissions). The most common was the choke executed from behind the opponent known in judo as *hadakajime* (16 times) (Kano, 1986; Koizumi, 1960; Takagaki & Sharp, 1998). The second one was a choke executed with the forearm against the windpipe while on top of the opponent (six times). The next was what is commonly referred to as guillotine choke or front headlock (four times). The fourth is the arm triangle choke (three times). Next was the triangle choke, known in judo as *sankakujime* (two times) (Kano, 1986; Koizumi, 1960). Last were three different kinds of neck cranks and three different chokes.

Pete Spratt attempting an armbar from the bottom position on Zach Light.

Another category of ground submissions was the arm lock, which accounted for 15 matches (8.5% of all matches and 23.8% of all ground submissions). In this division, the judo technique known as jujigatame (Kano, 1986; Koizumi, 1960; Takagaki & Sharp, 1998), or armbar, was the most common (11 times, eight of which occurred while in the guard position, two from the top mount, and one from the side mount). The next successful one was *udegarami* (Kano, 1986; Koizumi, 1960; Takagaki & Sharp, 1998), known in Brazilian jujutsu circles as the American Lock, which occurred four times (three times from a side mount and once from a top mount).

Above: Ricardo Almeida looking for a triangle choke during a match with Eugene Jackson.
Below: Carlos Newton applying a key-lock (aka "Kimura") against Pete Spratt

The last category of ground submissions was the leg lock, which ended seven matches (about 4% of all matches and slightly more than 11% of all ground submissions). Three of these leg-locks were knee bars, two were heel hooks, and two were Achilles locks. It is interesting to note that all but two of the leg locks were executed by fighters who had trained at the Lion's Den, a mixed martial arts school founded by Ken Shamrock, a veteran of the Japanese Pancrase association where leg-locks account for a much higher percentage of successful submissions (Shamrock, 1997).

In addition to submissions, many matches were won on the ground by striking (43 times, or 24.4% of all matches). Nearly all of the winning strikes were delivered by the fighter on top (either from a top, back, or side mount, with only very few from inside the guard). The favorite ways to strike were elbows, punches, and, when they were still legal, strikes using the head.

Frank Mir working an arm lock from his guard on Pete Williams.

Strikes delivered while standing ended 29 matches (16.5%). Eight were striking combinations (where no single blow was decisive, but rather the cumulative effect of three of four strikes in sequence forced the opponent to quit or caused a knockout). Seven were hooks (four right and three left directed at jaw, nose, or ear). Two were right crosses, two were knee strikes to the face, two were punches against a downed opponent, two were knee drops on a downed opponent's head (a technique that was among the first UFC officials outlawed), one was a roundhouse kick to a downed opponent's face, one was a foot stomp to a downed opponent's head, one was a foot stomp to a downed opponent's ribs (these 3 techniques also became illegal fairly soon), one was a roundhouse kick to the face (interestingly this was the only fight-ending high kick in 176 matches), one was a downward elbow, and one was a roundhouse kick to the thigh.

A guillotine choke on Keith Rockel, courtesy of Eugene Jackson.

Standing submissions only ended 4 matches (2.3%), and all were guillotine chokes (front headlocks).

A leg-lock attempt during UFC 24 (Neil Adams vs Ian Freeman).

Above: A rear naked choke (Bob Cook vs. Tiki Ghosen), one of the most common techniques in mixed martial arts competition.
Below: Carlos Newton, one of the most exciting fighters in UFC history, going for an armbar (jujigatame) on Bob Gilstrap.

Only one throw successfully ended a match (Frank Shamrock's spectacular knock out of Igor Zinoviev in Shamrock's first middleweight title defense). In this regard, it is useful to remember that this is a factor of the relatively soft surface on which the matches take place. On a harder surface, we could expect throws to have played a more important role. It is interesting to note that out of 176 matches, not a single one was won as a result of a joint lock executed while standing.

Technical Evolution

If we are to analyze how the relative importance of the winning techniques used by Ultimate Fighters has changed, we can begin to understand how the technical aspect of the sport has evolved.

One category that has certainly decreased in importance is striking on the ground. Whereas striking on the ground successfully ended 30.8% of all matches in UFC I through XI (including Ultimate Ultimate I and II), the percentage dropped to 23.5% between UFC XII and XV, and then dropped even further to 12.5% between UFC XVI and XII.

Ground submissions also decreased from 38.3% between UFC I and XI and 41.2% between UFC XII and XV to 27.1% in UFC XVI through XXII.

On the other hand, striking executed while standing up became increasingly more popular: from a mere 12.8% between UFC I and XI and 8.8% between UFC XII and XV to 29.2% between UFC XVI and XXII.

Throws and stand-up submissions account for such a small percentage of successful winning techniques that the change in percentage is not particularly indicative.

A key-lock (aka "Kimura") technique during UFC Brazil (Jermaine Andre vs. Lance Gibson).

Above: A classic armbar (Evan Tanner vs. Hommer Moore).
Below: Another key-lock technique during UFC Brazil
(Pete Williams vs. Tsuyoshi Kosaka).

The significance of these changes is especially enlightening. In the beginning, most people (including most martial artists and UFC fighters) believed that the technical key to martial arts proficiency rested on kicks and punches, and perhaps a few takedowns. The first UFC events proved this assumption wrong time and time again as most fights were won by good grapplers who regularly took their opponents to the ground, taking advantage of those trained in traditional styles emphasizing strikes who did not know what to do on the ground. For this reason, submissions and strikes on the ground decided most matches.

"The Ronin" Carlos Newton applying an armbar technique from the guard position on Bob Gilstrap.

Eventually, when shock and disbelief went away and most fighters began adjusting their game, a major technical change took place. No more would we see a fighter trained in only one style enter the octagon. Rather, much as Bruce Lee had advocated several decades earlier, different martial artists started borrowing from each other and ended up creating new fighting systems by taking the best from various arts and testing the techniques in combat (Lee, 1971, 1975; Bolelli, 2003). The UFC shortly became a laboratory for testing fighting efficiency. Most fighters found out that the best combination was to train in a few grappling styles such as Western freestyle and Greco-Roman wrestling, Brazilian jujutsu, judo, sambo, or submission wrestling and a couple of striking arts such as Western boxing and Muay Thai. Now that everyone began sharing a similar technical repertoire, mismatches became less common and dominating on the ground became more difficult. Even people who specialized in striking arts, in fact, knew enough about grappling to know how to sprawl well, make it difficult for the opponent to take them down, and avoid the simplest submissions if they did end up on the ground. The days when a grappler could take advantage of a naïve striker who knew nothing about groundfighting were over. Although ground submissions and to a lesser degree striking while on the ground were still very important, striking while standing up turned from a relatively minor aspect of the game to an equally important component.

The facts just outlined above are primarily responsible for the dramatic evolution of mixed martial arts during the formative decade of the 1990's.

Kevin Randleman on the wrong side of a triangle choke by Reanto Sobrol. This choke is obtained by the bottom player's leg applying pressure on one side of the neck and the top player's arm being squeezed tightly against his neck by the bottom player's other leg resulting in both carotid arteries being shut.

Bibliography

Anderson, S., & Jacques B. (1999). The development of sambo in Europe and America. *Journal of Asian Martial Arts*, 8(2): 20–41.

Barioli, C. (1996). *Il libro del judo*. Milano, Italy: De Vecchi Editore.

Bolelli, D. (2003). *On the warrior's path: The strategies of martial arts applied to daily life*. Berkeley, CA: Frog.

Kano, J. (1986). *Kodokan judo*. New York: Kodansha International.

Koizumi, G. (1960). *My study of judo*. New York: Sterling Publishing.

Krauss, E., & Aita, B. (2002). *Brawl: A behind-the-scenes look at mixed martial arts competition*. Toronto: ECW Press.

Lee, B. (1975). *The Tao of Jeet Kune Do*. Santa Clarita, CA: Ohara Publications.

Lee, B. (1971). Liberate yourself from classical karate. *Black Belt*.

Poliakoff, M. (1987). *Combat sports in the ancient world: Competition, violence, culture*. New Haven: Yale University Press.

Rutten, B., & Quadros, S. (2001). *Bas Rutten's big book of combat: Volume 1*. San Clemente, CA: Master Fighter.

Rutten, B., & Quadros, S. (2001). *Bas Rutten's big book of combat: Volume 2*. San Clemente, CA: Master Fighter.

Shamrock, K., & Hanner, R. (1997). *Inside the lion's den: The life and submission fighting system of Ken Shamrock*. Boston: Charles E. Tuttle Co.

Takagaki, S., & Sharp, H. (1998). *The techniques of judo*. Rutland, VT: Charles E. Tuttle.

Vale, B., & Jacobs, M. (2001). *Shootfighting: The ultimate fighting system*. Boulder: Paladin Press.

Note

[1] Statistics were derived by watching the tapes of every UFC event (numbers I through XXII, plus Ultimate Japan, Ultimate Brazil, U.U.I and U.U. II), noting the techniques utilized, timing the matches, then analyzing and recording the information provided for this article.

Varied Approaches to Grappling in Mixed Martial Arts Competition

by Daniele Bolelli, M.A.

Top left to right: Royce Gracie, Bas Rutten (courtesy B. Rutten).
Bottom left to right: Genki Sudo, and Carlos Newton.
All photographs courtesy of Dream Stage
Entertainment, except where noted.

Introduction

Since the early 1990's, the martial arts world has been revolutionized by the incredible success of grappling styles in mixed martial arts events such as the Ultimate Fighting Championship. Until that time, partly because of the way in which martial arts are represented in movies, the striking arts employing punching and high kicks represented the epitome of what martial arts fighting was all about. Mixed martial arts competitions gave popular imagination a wake-up call by proving over and over again that good grapplers could prevail over great strikers. Since success commands attention, grappling arts have experienced a renaissance in the last decade and have caught the interest of increasing numbers of peoples.

However, not all grappling arts are born equal. Many differences exist between the many martial arts styles that are often filed together under the heading of "grappling." Both in terms of their respective approaches to taking the opponent to the ground and in terms of the techniques used to finish the fight, grappling arts such as judo, Brazilian jujutsu, Greco-Roman wrestling, freestyle wrestling, sambo, shuai jiao, and submission wrestling differ tremendously from one another. To help clarify the vagueness that often accompanies any generic discussion of "grappling," this essay will highlight the different ways in which grappling techniques are currently used in mixed martial arts competition.

Takedowns

Although the focus of the essay will be on how different grappling styles go about finishing the matches, some words need to be said about how various grappling arts take the fight to the ground in the first place. Without effective takedown techniques, in fact, it would be virtually impossible for grapplers to be in a position to win a match.

Regarding their approaches to the takedown, grappling arts generally fall into one of two categories: 1) those that go immediately for a lower body takedown, such as freestyle wrestling, and 2) those that set up their throws from an upper body clinch, such as Greco-Roman wrestling, judo, and shuai jiao.

Those belonging to the first category require that grapplers "shoot," which means lunging for the opponent's legs from a distance, and usually finish the takedown with one of the many variations of the single- or double-leg techniques that are characteristic of freestyle wrestling. The advantage of this method is that the takedown can be initiated without any prior contact with the opponent, sometimes from several feet away. In cases where one's opponent is a good striker, this approach permits the grappler to attempt a takedown from outside the striking range, thereby taking the fight to the ground without having to engage in a stand-up striking battle at all. The main drawback to this approach is that the grappler may be vulnerable to a knee strike as he attempts to shoot. This is less common than one may imagine since the optimal range for a powerful knee strike is fairly short, so unless the knee hits the grappler with impeccable timing, it is very likely to do little or no damage. The second drawback to this approach is that if the opponent possesses good defensive wrestling skills and knows how to sprawl well, the grappler attempting the takedown may end up on the floor in an unfavorable position. Despite these problems, this method is often very successful and thus is very commonly used in mixed martial arts competition.

The second approach, setting up a takedown from a standing clinch, requires the competitor to find a way to bridge the initial distance to end up in an upper-body clinch. From this position, the grappler can employ leg sweeps or some crowd-pleasing high elevation throws, such as hip and shoulder throws and back-arching sacrifice throws. In addition to its aesthetic beauty, this approach has the advantage of offering an alternative way to take down an opponent whose excellent sprawling technique makes it hard to take him down by "shooting." Also, since the standing clinch is an extremely common position to end up in after an initial striking flurry, knowledge of takedown techniques from there becomes handy during most matches. The main drawback to this approach is that it requires the grappler to move within striking range before initiating the takedown. Against a good striker, this may result in being hit many times before ending up in a clinch. An additional drawback is that many throws (i.e. most hip and shoulder throws) that are initiated from the clinch require the grappler to turn his back to the opponent. If such a throw were to fail, it would put the person attempting it in an extremely bad position. Because of the high risk factor involved, many throws that are popular in Olympic judo occur only occasionally in mixed martial arts events.

The vast majority of grapplers are proficient in both methods. For example, even an artist of the upper body clinch such as Yoshida Hidehiko, the winner of an Olympic gold medal in judo, who usually likes to throw his opponent from the clinch, has employed double-leg takedowns in mixed martial arts competition. Most grapplers, however, tend to prefer one approach over the other.

Although the takedown is usually a means to an end and grapplers use it to bring the fight to the ground where they will then work toward a finishing move, occasionally the takedown can be used as a fight-finisher in itself. Fighters like Quinton Jackson, Tito Ortiz, and Frank Shamrock, have successfully ended some of their fights with particularly brutal takedowns. These fight-finishing takedowns usually see the grappler lifting the opponent in the air and then aiding gravity in slamming him on the ground for a knockout (KO) victory. This, however, is fairly rare since it is very difficult to knockout an opponent by throwing him to the floor if he is very skilled at falling and he happens to fall on the relatively soft floor of a ring. Grappling arts like Chinese shuaijiao place great emphasis on trying to finish the fight with a throw. However, since hardly any noteworthy shuaijiao fighter has participated in mixed martial arts events, not much can be said about their approach.

Finishing Techniques

Since takedowns and throws only rarely stop an opponent by themselves, grapplers win most of their matches on the floor. Three main approaches have emerged among grapplers to accomplish victory on the ground.

The first is the one that UFC and Pride FC veteran Mark Coleman baptized "ground and pound." This strategy consists in taking the opponent to the ground, gaining a dominant position (either top mount, back mount, half-guard, or even within an opponent's guard), and start raining strikes on the opponent to win by KO, technical knockout (TKO), or by the judges' decision. Even though victory is achieved by striking, the "ground and pound" strategy depends less on great striking skills and more on superior wrestling, which allows the grappler to maintain a dominant position on the ground. Even if the grappler's opponent is a much better striker than he is, once the grappler gains dominant position, he will inevitably win the exchange of strikes because he operates from a place where gravity and leverage work in his favor. No matter how good the striker may be, winning a match by striking from the bottom is next to impossible. This strategy is favored by fighters possessing exceptional wrestling ability but who are usually not as skilled in applying submissions (chokes and joint locks). Many freestyle and Greco-Roman wrestlers tend to favor this approach in mixed martial arts competition. Since these fighters often rely on their great physical strength, when they do attempt submissions they usually go for neck cranks and choking techniques that do not require great finesse.

Mark Coleman.
Courtesy of Dream Stage Entertainment.

The second strategy is the one commonly favored by fighters with backgrounds in Brazilian jujutsu and judo. Unlike fighters using the "ground and pound" strategy, Brazilian jujutsu and judo stylists do not rely on strikes as much as they do on submissions. In particular, they tend to focus on chokes (for example, the rear naked choke, guillotine choke, arm triangle choke, and triangle choke) and joint-locks against the elbow and/or shoulder (for example, the armbar [jujigatame] and several variations on the keylock). Also unlike people following the first strategy, followers of this second approach do not mind fighting from their backs, especially against opponents who are physically stronger. Many of their submissions, in fact, can be applied from the guard position when the fighter is on his back and his opponent is kneeling or standing between his legs). However, like followers of the first method, Brazilian jujutsu and judo fighters place great importance on improving their position, and ideally like to fight from a side, top, or back mount.

The third and last approach is the one often favored by fighters with backgrounds in submission wrestling and sambo. Among mixed martial arts competitors, the majority of Japanese grapplers who are not trained exclusively in judo belong to this category. Many of them have also studied judo and/or Brazilian jujutsu, but their grappling style is visibly different. Unlike "ground and pound" fighters and similar to judo and Brazilian jujutsu stylists, proponents of this third approach focus on submission techniques and do not mind fighting from their guard. Unlike judo and jujutsu stylists, however, these fighters place little or no emphasis on position, but rather follow a "do-or-die" philosophy that makes them willing to give up an advantageous position to attempt a submission. In their quest to force their opponent to submit from every imaginable position, some of these fighters experiment (sometimes successfully) with some very unorthodox techniques. Rumina Sato's flying armbar and flying triangle choke victories are perfect examples of this. Both techniques, in fact, are usually only attempted from certain positions on the ground. Sato, on the other hand, thought nothing of initiating them by jumping onto the opponent from a standing position. In addition to the chokes and arm locks that are common among judo and Brazilian jujutsu stylists, proponents of this third approach include leg locks (heel hooks, ankle locks, toe holds, calf slicers, and knee bars) in their arsenal of submissions. The considerable attention that these fighters pay to leg locks explains how different their strategy is from that of those promoting the second approach. Whereas it is possible to attempt chokes and arm locks—the staple submissions of judo and Brazilian jujutsu fighters—while maintaining a dominant position, to attempt a leg lock, a grappler has to take a gamble since he has to give up the dominant position. At that point, either the submission will be successful and he will win the fight or more likely he will end up in a neutral or even a disadvantageous position. The submission wrestlers' willingness to take this risk is not shared by most judo and Brazilian jujutsu practitioners, a fact that is underscored by how until very recently the latter would almost never attempt foot locks (Gracie & Peligro, 2003: 2).

To illustrate and back the divisions outlined above, let us now use as case studies the careers of twelve successful mixed martial arts fighters (four for each category). Analyzing how they obtained their victories will offer empirical background for our model.

GROUND AND POUND

The four masters of the "ground and pound" chosen as examples are former UFC light-heavyweight champion Tito Ortiz (whose main background is in freestyle wrestling), current UFC light-heavyweight and former UFC heavyweight champion Randy Couture (Greco-Roman wrestling), UFC and Pride tournaments champion Mark Coleman (freestyle wrestling), and UFC and Pride veteran Mark Kerr. Here is a breakdown of how each of these four fighters achieved their career victories.

- **Tito Ortiz, 10 victories:** Five from TKOs when the referee stopped the matches as Ortiz was hitting the opponent from a dominant position on the ground, one from a towel being thrown in between rounds, two by judges' decision, one by KO from a slam, and only one by submission through a neck crank.

- **Randy Couture, 13 victories:** Six decisions, six TKOs because of striking from a dominant position on the ground, and one rear naked choke.

- **Mark Coleman, 13 victories:** Five TKOs because of effective striking from a dominant position on the ground, three decisions, two towels being thrown, two chokes, and one neck crank.

- **Mark Kerr, 13 victories:** Three TKOs from strikes from a dominant position on the ground, two by disqualification of the opponent, two by decision, one KO from stand-up striking, one rear naked choke, one neck crank, two shoulder locks (Kimura and American lock), and one by pressing the chin into the eye while on the ground (a technique that became illegal in mixed martial arts competition shortly thereafter).

When taken as a whole, these fighters' 49 victories seem to follow a pattern. Only 20.4% come from submissions, the only submissions were neck cranks (three), chokes (four), variations on the keylock (two), and the unusual chin to the eye. Many of the bread-and-butter techniques of submission fighters, such as the armbar, the triangle choke, or any type of leg-lock, are completely absent.

Left: Mark Kerr. Courtesy of Dream Stage Entertainment.
Right: Randy Couture. Courtesy of the Ultimate Fighting Championships.

Above: Ortiz vs. Cote. Courtesy of the Ultimate Fighting Championships.

Above: Randy Couture. Courtesy of the Ultimate Fighting Championships.
Below: Couture vs. Ortiz. Courtesy of the Ultimate Fighting Championships.

By contrast, almost half of their victories, 44.9%, come either from TKOs or towels being thrown in as a result of effective striking on the ground. Of these victories, 26.5% more came from effective striking on the ground when the strikes were not enough to force a referee's stoppage but were crucial in gaining the judges' decision. Only one fight ended by KO because of strikes delivered while standing up, and also only one ended by KO because of a throw; two ended because of disqualification. As we can see, these fighters use grappling mostly as a mean to control the fight on the ground and win by striking. Although submissions are part of their arsenal, they are only a secondary strategy, and even then, only few basic kinds of submissions are employed.

Antonio Rodrigo Nogueria.
Courtesy of Dream Stage Entertainment.

BRAZILIAN JUJUTSU

Helio and Royce Gracie approaching ringside.
Courtesy of Dream Stage Entertainment.

The four Brazilian jujutsu experts in our survey are former Pride FC heavyweight champion Antonio Rodrigo Nogueira, UFC pioneer Royce Gracie, the legendary Rickson Gracie, and former UFC welterweight champion and Pride FC veteran Carlos Newton.

- **Antonio Rodrigo Nogueira, 24 victories:** Eight armbars (jujigatame), three triangle chokes, one keylock, one neck crank, one rear naked choke, one arm triangle choke, two "anaconda" chokes, six decisions, and one KO from a punch delivered while standing.
- **Royce Gracie, 12 victories:** Three rear naked chokes, two chokes using his own or the opponent's gi, one triangle choke, three armbars, one TKO from striking on the ground, one decision, and one towel being thrown in.
- **Rickson Gracie, 9 victories:** Five rear naked chokes, two armbars, two TKOs because of striking on the ground. Many more victories are attributed to Rickson Gracie, but almost all of them were fought at local events or in private challenges and are usually not recognized.
- **Carlos Newton, 12 victories:** Six armbars, one Kimura, one triangle choke, one headlock choke, and three judges' decisions.

Royce Gracie on the matt and posing for portrait.
Courtesy of Dream Stage Entertainment.

If we analyze their cumulative 57 victories, the picture that emerges is very different from the one we saw with the first group of grapplers. An overwhelming 73.7% of them are the result of submissions (as opposed to the 20.4% for the first group). Out of these submission techniques, the most common is the armbar (which ended 33.3% of their matches), followed by the rear naked choke (which ended 15.8% of the matches), and the triangle choke (8.8% of the matches). Among the other submissions employed are many different types of chokes (including the highly unusual "anaconda" choke) and shoulder locks. Not only do the Brazilian jujutsu fighters rely more on submission techniques than the first group of wrestlers, but they also use a much wider range. It is also interesting to note that the armbar and the triangle choke, which are respectively the first and third most common techniques used by these fighters, were never used by the wrestlers to win. Among the other victories won by these jujutsu fighters, 17.5% were obtained through judges' decisions; only 5.3% are the result of striking on the ground (as opposed to 44.9% in the case of the wrestlers); one was the result of a standing KO; and one because of an opponent giving up. This statistical comparison clearly underscores how these two groups of fighters use their grappling skills in completely different ways.

Above: Carlos Newton locks his opponent.

Right: Newton shown wearing a championship belt. Courtesy of the Ultimate Fighting Championships.

Rickson Gracie. Courtesy of Dream Stage Entertainment.

SUBMISSION WRESTLING

The third group of fighters is represented by Pride FC legend Kazushi Sakuraba, the Dutch three-time King of Pancrase and former UFC heavyweight champion Bas Rutten, the highly flamboyant Genki Sudo (a veteran of UFC, Pancrase, Rings, and K-1), and Shooto superstar Rumina Sato.

- **Kazushi Sakuraba, 16 victories:** Six armbars, two Kimuras, one kneebar, one Achilles lock, one rear naked choke, three judges' decisions, one towel being thrown in when the opponent couldn't continue, and one being forfeited by the opponent.
- **Bas Rutten, 27 victories:** Four standing KOs, five standing TKOs, three toe holds, two heel hooks, one kneebar, three rear naked chokes, one arm triangle choke, one neck crank, four guillotine chokes, one armbar, and two judges' decisions.
- **Genki Sudo, 10 victories:** Two rear naked chokes, one triangle choke, two armbars, one heel hook, one Achilles lock, two TKOs from striking on the ground, and one decision.
- **Rumina Sato, 21 victories:** Seven armbars, one flying armbar, one flying reverse triangle choke, one triangle choke, two rear naked chokes, three heel hooks, one toe hold, one kneebar, one calf slicer, one TKO from punching, and two decisions.

Left: Bas Rutten. Photo Courtesy of B. Rutten.
Right: Genki Sudo Courtesy of DreamStage Entertainment.

Most of these 74 career victories (70.2%) came from submission techniques, a similar percentage to that seen for the Brazilian jujutsu fighters. Clearly there are some similarities between the kinds of submissions the two groups used. Armbars are the most common kind of submission for both (33.3% of the Brazilian jujutsu fighters' victories, and 21.6% of the submission wrestlers). Rear naked chokes are also prevalent among both (15.8% for the Brazilian jujutsu fighters, and 10.8% for the submission wrestlers.) Furthermore, fighters in both groups have used triangle chokes, Kimura shoulder locks, neck cranks, and arm triangle chokes to finish a match.

However, there are also major differences. Whereas the four Brazilian jujutsu fighters have never won a single match by leg lock, leverages against the legs gave the submission wrestlers 21.6% of their victories (six heel hooks, four toe holds, three kneebar, two Achilles hold, one calf slicer). This disparity clearly constitutes a very significant difference between the two groups. Also, the fact that submission wrestlers won some of their fights thanks to very risky techniques such as flying armbars and flying reverse triangle chokes shows their willingness to pursue submissions from most unusual positions. Among the submission wrestlers' other victories, a fairly small percentage (4%) comes from TKO from striking on the ground (the percentage was 5.3% for the Brazilian jujutsu fighters and 44.9% for the "ground and pound" wrestlers), and 10.8% from judges' decisions (compared to 17.5% for the jujutsu fighters and 26.5% for the wrestlers). Bas Rutten's four standing KOs and five standing TKOs are an anomaly since Rutten was first and foremost a kickboxer who became an excellent submission wrestler but who—unlike most other grappling specialists—could win many fights by striking from a standing position.

Genki Sudo gets wrapped up. Courtesy of Dream Stage Entertainment.

The above case studies provide concrete backing to the idea that there are three distinct main approaches to using grappling in a mixed martial arts match. Enough statistical differences support this claim. Like all rules, this one has its exceptions. There are grapplers, in fact, who do not easily fit into any of these three categories, but rather seem to mix these approaches in a very balanced way. Pride FC heavyweight champion Emelianenko Fedor, for example, is a sambo specialist and thereby a submission wrestler by training. In his mixed martial arts career so far, he has proven to be one of the best "ground and pound" experts in the world. Furthermore, he has achieved several victories with the submission techniques that are typical of Brazilian jujutsu. Fighters such as former UFC welterweight champion B.J. Penn and Shooto champion Hayato Sakurai provide more examples of great grapplers who seem to escape being pigeonholed in any neat scheme. Maybe these eclectic grapplers who are equally versed in different approaches will be the norm in the future, but for now, the majority of grapplers who enter a mixed martial art event tend to fall into one of the three categories outlined above.

Bibliography

Alter, J. (1992). *The wrestler's body: Identity and ideology in north India.* Berkeley: University of California Press.

Barioli, C. (1988/1996). *Il libro del judo.* De Vecchi Editore: Milano.

Bolelli, D. (2003). *On the warrior's path: Philosophy, fighting and martial arts mythology.* Berkeley: Frog Ltd.

Bolelli, D. (2003). Mixed martial arts: A technical analysis of the Ultimate Fighting Championship in its formative years. *Journal of Asian Martial Arts, 12*(3): 40–51.

Cartmell, T. (1996). *Principles, analysis, and application of effortless combat throws.* Pacific Grove, CA: High View Publications.

Cartmell, T., & Beneville, E. (2002). *Passing the guard: Brazilian jiu-jitsu details and techniques Volume 1.* Costa Mesa, CA: Grappling Arts Publications.

Draeger, D., & Inokuma, I. (1966). *Weight training for championship judo.* Tokyo: Kodansha International.

Jacques, B., & Anderson, S. (1999). The development of sambo in Europe and America. *Journal of Asian Martial Arts,* 8(2), 20–40.

Gentry, C. (2002). *No holds barred: The story of ultimate fighting.* Ramsbottom, England: Milo Books Ltd.

Gracie, R., & Danaher, J. (2003). *Mastering jiujitsu.* Champaign, IL: Human Kinetics.

Gracie, R. & Gracie, R. with Peligro, K. & Danaher, J. (2001). *Brazilian jiu-jitsu: Theory and technique.* Montpelier, VT: Invisible Cities Press.

Gracie, R., & Peligro, K. (2003). *Brazilian jiu-jitsu: Submission grappling techniques.* Montpelier, VT: Invisible Cities Press.

Harrington, P. (2002). *Judo basics: Principles, rules and rankings.* Tokyo: Kodansha International.

Hunt, B. (1964). *Greco-Roman wrestling.* New York: The Ronald Press.

Kano, J. (1986). *Kodokan judo.* New York: Kodansha International.

Koizumi, G. (1960). *My study of judo.* New York: Sterling Publishing Co.

Krauss, E., & Aita, B. (2002). *Brawl: A behind-the-scenes look at mixed martial arts competition.* Toronto: ECW Press.

Kudo, K. (1967). *Dynamic judo.* Tokyo: Japan Publications Trading Co.

LeBelle, G., & Coughran, L. (1962). *The handbook of judo.* New York: Thomas Nelson and Sons.

Liang, S., & Ngo, T. (1997). *Chinese fast wrestling for fighting: The art of san shou kuai jiao.* Jamaica Plain: YMAA Publication Center.

Martell, W. (1993). *Greco-Roman wrestling.* Champaign, IL: Human Kinetics Publishers.

Mysnyk, M., Davis, B., & Simpson, B. (1994). *Winning wrestling moves*. Champaign, IL: Human Kinetics Publishers.

Peligro, K. (2003). *The Gracie way: An illustrated history of the world's greatest martial arts family*. Montpelier, VT: Invisible Cities Press.

Rutten, B., & Quadros, S. (2001). *Bas Rutten's big book of combat, Volume 1*. San Clemente, CA: Master Fighter.

Rutten, B., & Quadros, S. (2001). *Bas Rutten's big book of combat, Volume 2*. San Clemente, CA: Master Fighter.

Shamrock, K., & Hanner, R. (1997). *Inside the lion's den: The life and submission fighting system of Ken Shamrock*. Boston: Charles E. Tuttle Co.

Smith, R. (1958). *A complete guide to judo: Its story and practice*. Rutland, VT: Charles E. Tuttle.

Takagaki, S., & Sharp, H. (1957/1998). *The techniques of judo*. Rutland, VT: Charles E. Tuttle.

Vale, B., & Jacobs, M. (2001). *Shootfighting: The ultimate fighting system*. Boulder, CO: Paladin Press.

Van De Walle, R. (1993). *Pick-ups*. London: Ippon Books Ltd.

Weng, D. (1984). *Fundamentals of shuai chiao: The ancient Chinese fighting art*. Taipei: Chinese Culture University.

The Choke:
The Ultimate Finishing Technique
by Andrew Zerling, B.S.

Rear Naked Choke

Renzo Gracie finalizes his partner, Andrew Zerling, with the powerful rear naked choke.
The choke is also called *mata leão* (lion killer) in Brazilian jujutsu.
All photos courtesy of A. Zerling and R. Gracie.

Introduction

Chokes or strangulation techniques (*shimewaza*) have been an integral part of most grappling martial arts since the dawn of hand-to-hand combat. When performed properly, the choke or strangulation renders your opponent temporarily unconscious for 10–20 seconds if the pressure is released promptly after they go under. Severe brain damage or death can occur if pressure from the choke is applied too long, obstructing either the passage of air via the windpipe, or blood flow via the carotid artery feeding the brain. Although this technique may seem too dangerous for routine practice, no deaths have occurred from shimewaza in over one hundred years of documented judo history of competition. For many reasons, the choke is the preferred finishing technique of the Brazilian jujutsu (BJJ) practitioner. Carlos Gracie Jr., son of the founding father of BJJ, indicated that the choke cleanly and definitely ends the fight. Gracie also mentions that many tough fighters, especially the Japanese fighters, will continue to fight even with a broken arm from a good arm lock. The idea of putting your opponent temporarily to sleep with a choke is that it leaves no question of who won the fight. Of course, if your opponent signals defeat by "tapping" in response to a good choke, you can stop the technique before unconsciousness occurs. This article discusses the choke from a technical, ethical, and historical perspective with numerous references. In this article we will mainly use the term "choke" as preferred in BBJ nomenclature.

The Choking Technique

According to the *Kodokan New Japanese-English Dictionary of Judo* (2000: 117) shimewaza (strangulation techniques) are: "Techniques in which the opponent is strangled by applying pressure to parts of his neck." In judo, shimewaza can be a carotid artery attack that stops blood flow to the brain, or any attack that stops the air supply. Old Japanese jujutsu shimewaza had less restrictive rules for safety, and also included shimewaza for the diaphragm (*dojime*), and the face, and for the neck. In BJJ the term "choke" is meant to describe all techniques that can put your opponent to sleep from lack of blood flow to the brain or lack of air supply.

The most efficient chokes are carotid artery chokes. They take effect more rapidly (approx. 10 seconds) and are less dangerous than other types of chokes. According to Dr. Karl Koiwai (1987): "Neck pressure of 250mm Hg or 5kg of rope tension is required to occlude carotid arteries." Judo and BJJ employ carotid artery chokes as the most common type of choking maneuver because of their ease in performing, relative safety, and efficiency. Chokes that stop the air flow, such as wind pipe (trachea) compression, are used more as a pain-inducing maneuver than a sleep-inducing technique. Trunk squeezing with the legs (dojime) can cause unconsciousness if done properly, but the kidneys and other internal organs can be damaged. Attacking the wind pipe with a choke is still allowed in judo contests, but dojime is illegal. A lesser known variant of shimewaza is smothering the face and nose to block the air to the lungs. While this may be effective in a street fight, it is disallowed in judo contests. Judo contests have many more safety measures than no-nolds-barred (NHB) contests. Understanding and comparing the safety measures in each of these sports helps gauge the general risk of each technique.

One of the key requirements of a good choke is to take total control of the opponent's body. In today's NHB events most chokes are done from dominant ground positions. A high success rate of submissions come from dominant ground positions. Ideally, the choke should be performed from a dominant ground position (i.e., the back, mount, side control, guard). Once you have this dominant ground position you have to maintain it while you are trying to choke the opponent. The longer you maintain the dominant position the more fatigued the opponent will be trying to escape from his poor position. This will increase your chances of a submission. With a dominant ground position you can control the opponent more efficiently with your hips and legs than he can with his own. You can then recruit your whole body into the technique, especially your legs which are one of the strongest parts of the body and are not needed for standing when positioned on the ground. Remember that the opponent will be thrashing around attempting to escape the choke. It is possible to obtain a submission from a less dominant position, but the percentage rate for success is lower. Therefore, good positional ground grappling skills are essential for obtaining most submissions (Gracie, et al., 2001, 2003).

Flexible and sensitive wrists are essential for a choke to be performed properly. Proper use of the arms and wrists is as important as the dominant ground position using the legs to control the opponent. Each wrist plays its own specific role in the application of a tight choke. Just tugging at the *gi* (judo uniform) is insufficient. Choking requires dexterity and finesse.

The choke is the most often used finishing maneuver in a NHB fight to obtain a submission. For instance, in the illustrious fight careers of some of the top Gracie family NHB fighters (i.e., Rickson, Royce, and Renzo), most of their victories from submission come from various choking techniques from the ground. The only standing choke that appears to be able to put the opponent down consistently in NHB is the front naked choke or guillotine. This choke works well when you are being tackled by the legs via the front from a wrestling takedown. The lowering of the opponent's head for the shot at the legs usually leaves the neck exposed. Many wrestlers have been submitted this way. Nevertheless the focus of the choking techniques should be from ground positions as discussed earlier.

Mounted Cross Choke

This technique is a carotid artery strangle. It can also be done from the guard and knee on the belly. The hand position is the key to this move, so the photo sequence is focused on the hand movements.

A-1 Renzo Gracie is mounted on his partner, Andrew Zerling, and feeds his right hand four fingers into the collar.

A-2 The right hand grip is as deep as possible, to the middle of the back of the neck.

A-3 Gracie then grasps the top of the cloth near the neck above his partner's shoulder.

A-4 The jujutsu expert then bases out with his head and neck to prevent a possible roll off attempt. To finish off the cross choke, he spread his elbows out tight to his ribs while strongly gripping the cloth.

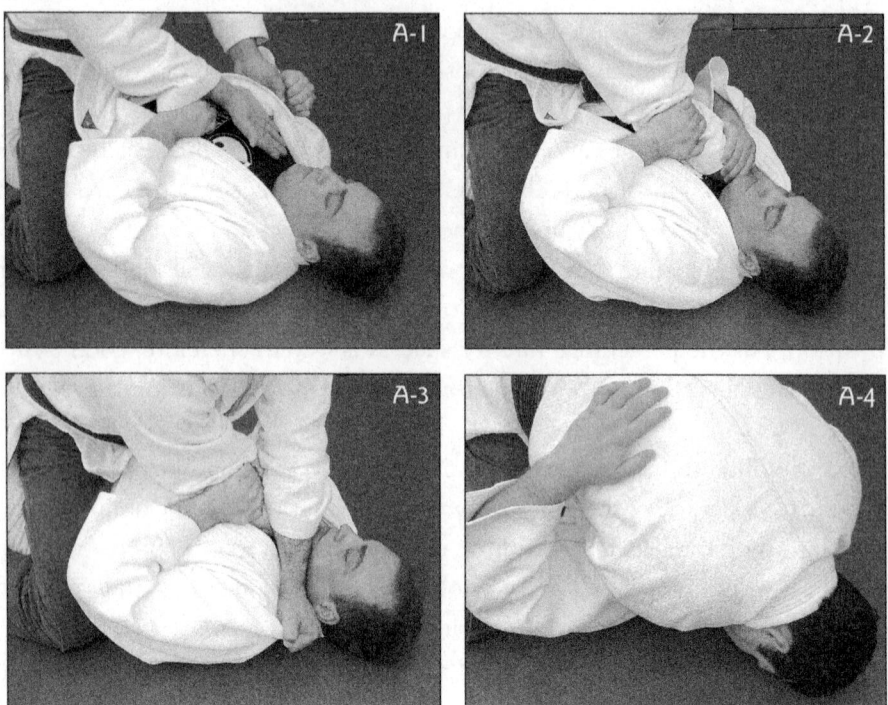

LeBelle and Coughran (1962) state that chokes are useful against adversaries that are resistant to pain for some reason (i.e. drug/alcohol use and/or mental state). The momentary stoppage of blood to the brain will stop anyone. Even a kick to the groin or a strike to the eyes or throat may be insufficient to thwart a highly determined combatant. When it comes to choking, no oxygen supply to the brain means no more fight.

The *U.S. Army Combatives Field Manual* from 1971 to 2001 chronicles a distinct evolution in the way chokes are applied. As of 1971, North America had not yet been introduced to the Gracie jujutsu system, which deals mainly with highly effective one-on-one ground fighting, and so the 1971 edition contained almost no chokes from ground position. In the 1971 manual, there was probably judo influence, with many large throwing techniques and few ground submissions.

The 2001 edition of the manual contains more ground submissions, including those utlizing chokes from the mounted position. No "hold downs" (*osaekomi*) are shown, since on the battlefield there is usually no reason to simply contain your foe, when you must swiftly incapacitate or kill them.

Front Shoulder Choke

This choke is an excellent one to employ in a street fight. Your opponent cannot counter-attack by biting or eye gouging, since his teeth and arms are trapped away from you. This choke can be done from the guard, the mount, and side control.

B-1 Renzo Gracie is on bottom with his partner trapped in his closed guard. His partner tries to choke him with one arm while trying to pass his guard.

B-2 Gracie elevates his pelvis which takes the pressure of his partner's choke away. At the same time the jujutsu expert controls his partner's choking arm with both of his arms.

B-3 While controlling his partner's elbow, Gracie then, brings his partner forward to him by using his pelvis and legs. Gracie then gets to the side of his partner's body and at the same time deeply wraps his right arm around the neck.

B-4 The jujutsu expert then finalizes things with the highly effective blood choke by grabbing his left arm bicep with his deeply sunk in right arm. To apply the choke, Gracie squeezes his elbows together.

Utilizing or Not Utilizing the Gi for Chokes

Shimewaza are clearly divided in to two categories: Shimewaza with the cloth and "naked" chokes (without the cloth). Use of the gi in grappling training traces back to Japanese tradition. This may stem from the fact that the Japanese wear kimonos in their daily life and the kimono is similar to the current jujutsu/judo style gi. Kashiwazaki (1992) indicated that certain strangulation techniques developed in a large part in connection with the Japanese kimono. Also the Japanese geo-political "isolation" from the rest of the world for hundreds of years may have let their martial arts develop in different directions.

Judo can be regarded as the first modern grappling system to make use of the kimono exclusively. Because of the sporting rules made for judo, other techniques based on grabbing the gi were used more often compared to traditional jujutsu techniques. To quote Kashiwazaki (1992: 13): "The development of judo as a sport had a dramatic effect on the application of the strangles. Techniques such as *namijujijime* (normal cross gi choke) and *gyakujujijime* (reverse cross gi choke) from the 'on-top' position (mount) became less effective than hold-downs (*osaekomi*). Other techniques such as *okurierijime* and *katahajime* applied from behind became more useful, and remained so as judo became an Olympic sport."

Rear Gi Choke

C-1 Renzo Gracie has his partner's back and begins the sliding collar strangle by opening up the collar with his left hand.

C-2 Gracie then feeds the collar to his right hand. His right hand grabs the collar deeply.

C-3 Then his left hand takes the right lower collar to set up the strangle.

C-4 To finalize the choke, the jiu-jistu expert slides his right hand across his partner's throat and pulls down with his left hand to keep the collar tightly around the neck for this carotid artery strangle. The key to this choke, as with most chokes, is that Gracie keeps his wrists flexible to gain the proper leverage. Note how Gracie controls his partner's body by using his legs like hooks. This is critical as his partner will be using his whole body while trying to escape.

More recently, Brazilian jujutsu (BJJ), another kimono oriented grappling system, has emerged in popularity because of its combat effectiveness. BJJ and judo are very closely related, since both are derivatives of traditional Japanese jujutsu. The combat focus of BJJ has changed the use of the gi somewhat. Hold downs are not considered fight ending maneuvers as in competition judo. The BJJ artist's usual goal is to finish the fight with his myriad of submissions.

In judo competition, "giving your back" is considered strategically good if it avoids a hold down, but in BJJ, it is the worst position to be in. You cannot defend against strikes when your back is to the opponent. In BJJ, you should always try to face the opponent. The idea of positional dominance changes the focus of BJJ submissions into one involving face-to-face finishing holds, as compared to judo's attack to the back (turtle position). For example, the cross gi chokes (*jujijime*) from the on-top mount position are often downplayed in judo, but is commonly used as a finishing maneuver in BJJ (Gracie, et al., 2001, 2003).

Guard Front Triangle

This is the carotid artery choke Renzo Gracie's cousin Royce Gracie used to submit Dan Severn.

D-3 Renzo Gracie is on bottom with his partner in his closed guard. He controls one of his partner's wrists.

D-2 The jujutsu expert then pushes the controlled arm to his partner's belly while opening his guard.

D-3 Gracie's left leg is posting on his partner's right hip while his calve of his right leg sinks in deeply perpendicular to his partner's neck. At the same time his upper body is shifting to his right with the help of his posted left foot on the hip.

D-4 Gracie then tucks his right ankle under his left knee to create a tight leg triangle. All throughout this technique Gracie controls his partner's right arm with either one or both of his hands. To choke his partner out, the jujutsu expert tries to bring his knees together, elevates his hips and lowers his legs.

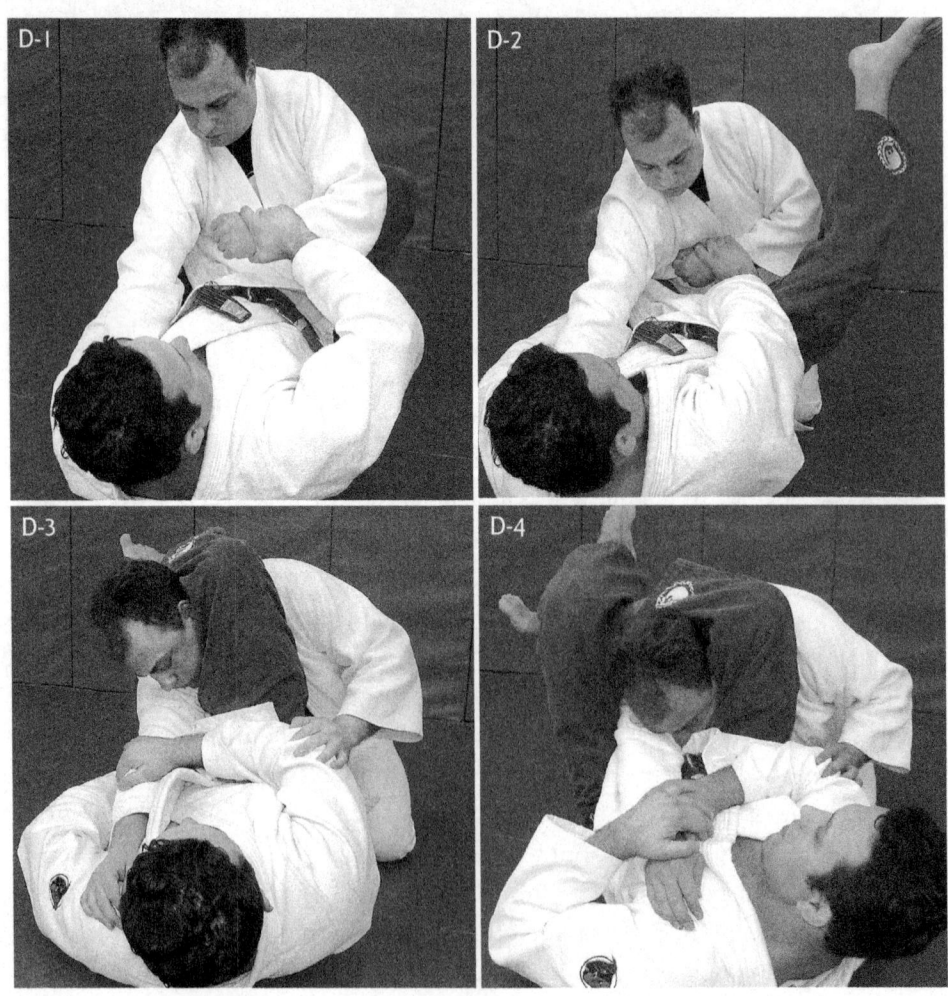

There are many hundreds of variations of gi or cloth strangulations in a gi-oriented ground grappling system such as BJJ, and so, if your opponent wears a gi, there is a good chance that the cloth can be used for a choke. When gi clad opponents faced BJJ experts in NHB, they were very often defeated by a cloth choke, i.e. Royce vs. Ichihara, Royce vs. Pardoel, and Renzo vs. Spijkers.

Naked chokes (no gi) are generally more difficult to apply than gi chokes because the gi provides a handle and lever. Gi chokes are important to know, but are of little use if the opponent does not wear a shirt. Performing naked chokes is also more difficult when the opponent wears a gi, because the gi creates some friction that keeps your arms or legs from sinking tightly into place. Therefore, in judo for instance, where gis are worn always in competition, most chokes are with the gi. Since BJJ is more often practiced without wearing a gi, gi chokes are not possible at this level of combat (Gracie & Danahar, 2003).

One of the more powerful chokes is the triangle choke (*sankakujime*) with the legs. The triangle choke does not require use of the cloth. It can be done from a number of different positions, with the major examples being the front triangle, side triangle, reverse triangle, and rear triangle. Since the leg triangle is not done standing, the triangle with the legs has become the signature ground submission technique in BJJ. The leg triangle is unlike many other chokes which can also be done while standing, like cross chokes and certain rear chokes. Competition judo does make use of the leg triangle for submission when ground fighting, but its main signature is the perfect throw for the winning point (*ippon*). BJJ proponents believe that the throw or takedown gets you to the ground where the fight is just beginning. BJJ's use of the leg triangle has finished many sport and NHB competitions.

The first mainstream martial arts introduction of the leg triangle choke was in the 1994 Ultimate Fighting Championship IV (Revenge of the Warriors). It was a classic match up between the expert submission artist, Royce Gracie, and the massively strong wrestler, Dan Severn. While Gracie was tightening the front leg triangle from bottom in the guard on Severn, most of the audience actually thought Severn had the advantage, but then Severn quickly tapped out. Severn outweighed Gracie by a very large margin, although with the technical use of his long powerful legs against a weak part of the wrestler's neck, Gracie gained the upper hand and won.

The details of the mechanics for submission techniques (i.e., chokes, arm locks, leg locks) and positioning (i.e., guard passing, mount escaping) are critically important for success in a ground fight. But the real secret of applying the techniques is the training method. Drilling the details of the moves with a partner without resistance in the beginning is important for proper mechanics, and then grappling with an uncooperative resisting partner is necessary to test your skills.

With resistance grappling, skills can be improved in ways that cannot be done from drills alone. These lessons learned, and the physical and spiritual conditioning from full resistance grappling make one a much more formidable fighter (Gracie, et al, 2001).

Side Control Sleeve Choke

With this choke, your partner doesn't really need to wear a gi jacket to be effective.

E-3 Renzo Gracie is in the cross side position. Gracie begins to clear his partner's right arm with his left arm.
E-2 Gracie clears the right arm, which now cannot be used to counter the choke.
E-3 The jujutsu expert then grips his left arm's sleeve with four fingers inside.
E-4 Gracie encircles his opponent's neck with his arms.
E-5 He is now in position to choke with his forearms against the sides of his partner's neck.
E-6 Gracie partially straightens his arm and pushes against the neck to constrict the blood flow.

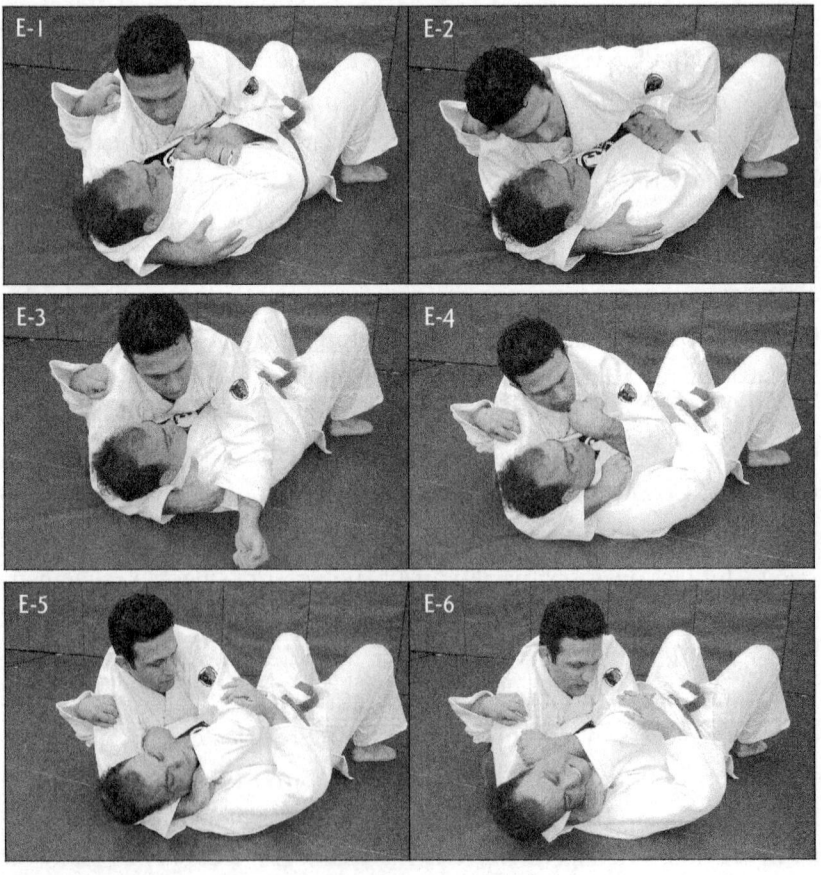

Ethics in Utilizing Choking Techniques

The use of chokes to subdue an adversary is also considered an ethical way of dealing with violent attacks. In Uyenishi's book (1905), he readily mentions that it is much more humane to put someone to sleep with a strangulation than to break joints or strike repeatedly. If the choke is applied properly the opponent will awaken practically unharmed from his sleep in about 20 seconds. A hundred years ago, it was realized that the choke was the ground technique of choice for the ethical treatment of your opponent.

Conclusion

The choke technique has a high success rate in NHB competitions, and it can be practiced safely with proper training. Being proficient in both gi and no gi chokes is essential to a well-rounded grappling arsenal. BJJ is well-known for training in both of these two methods, judo is almost always trained with the kimono. Jimmy Pedro, World Champion and Olympic Medalist in judo, wrote (2001: 61): "Practice judo occasionally with someone who is not wearing a judo gi to prepare yourself for the real-world situation in which your attacker is not wearing a jacket." Choking is also an ethical way to end a fight, since it causes minimal damage to your adversary if done properly. If you are not already familiar, you should acquire knowledge of chokes as an ultimate finishing technique.

Bibliography

Gracie, R., & Danaher, J. (2003). *Mastering jujitsu.* Champaign, IL: Human Kinetics.

Gracie, R., Gracie, R., Peligro, K., & Danaher, J. (2001). *Brazilian jiu-jitsu theory and technique.* Montpelier, VT: Invisible Cities Press.

Headquarters Department of the Army: Combatives, Field Manual No. 21–150. Washington, D.C.: Headquarters Department of the Army, 1971.

Headquarters Department of the Army: Combatives, Field Manual No. 3–25.150. Washington, D.C.: Headquarters Department of the Army, 2002. http://www.globalsecurity.org/military/library/policy/army/fm/3–25–150.

Kashiwazaki, K. (1992). *Shimewaza.* Bristol, UK: Ippon Books.

Kawamura, T., & Daigo, T. (2000). *Kodokan new Japanese-English dictionary of judo.* Tokyo: The Foundation of Kodokan Judo Institute.

Koiwai, M., & Karl, E. (March 1987). Anatomy of a choke. *Journal of Forensic Science.*

LeBell, G., & Coughran, L. (1962). *The handbook of judo*. New York: Cornerstone Library.

Pedro, J., & Drubin, W. (2001). *Judo techniques and tactics*. Champaign, IL: Human Kinetics.

Uyenishi, S. (1997). *The text-book of ju-jutsu as practised in Japan*. Dragon Associates. Reprint of 1905 edition by Atheletic Publications, London.

The Arm Lock:
The Technique of Control
by Andrew Zerling, B.S.

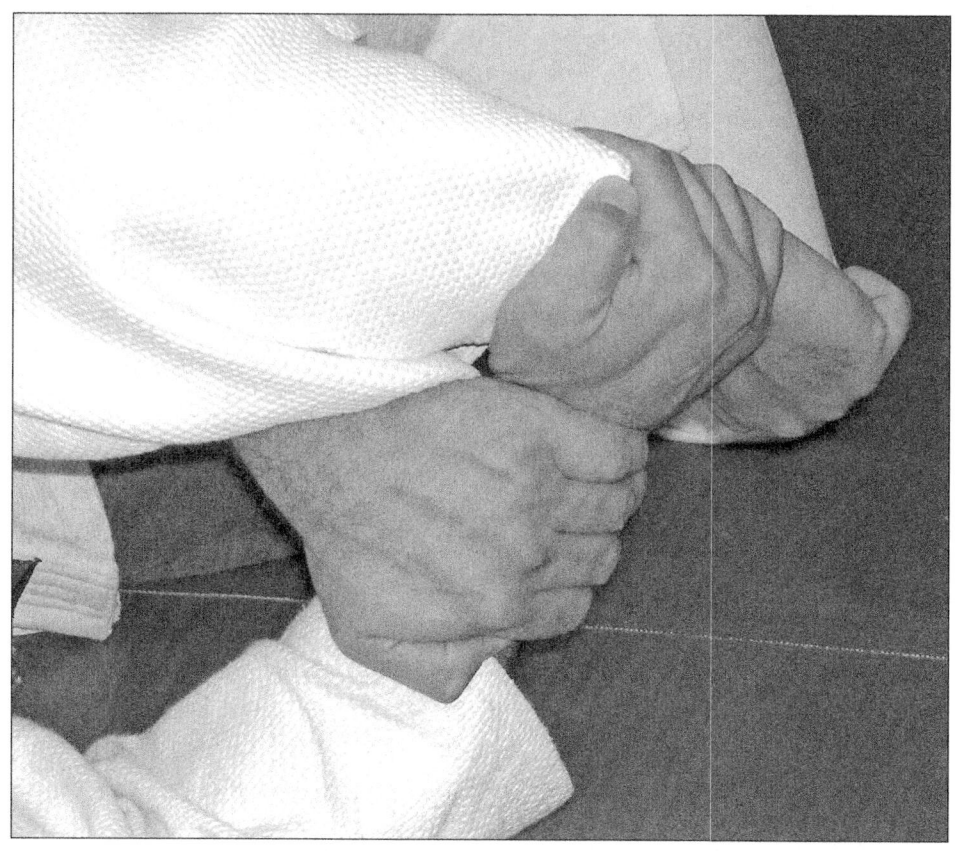

Close-up of the Kimura grip.
All photos courtesy of A. Zerling and R. Gracie.

Introduction

When most martial artists think of a joint lock they will assume it is an arm lock. Practically all grappling martial arts exploit the inherent anatomical weakness of their opponent's arms. In competition judo the only joint allowed to be manipulated is the elbow joint. Other martial arts, such as aikido, specialize in wrist, finger and other arm locks. Even with the broad submission capabilities of Brazilian jujutsu (BJJ), the arm lock is one of the preferred finishing holds of the BJJ artist. This article presents a brief history and discusses the application of the infamous arm lock: the technique of control.

The Arm Lock Technique

The history of the arm lock can be traced back into Asiatic history. Most of Western wrestling believed the arm lock to be an unsportsmanlike maneuver. In traditional Japanese jujutsu, arm locks were preferably performed with the opponent face down, giving you more control, making it harder for him to produce a weapon or strike with his free arm. The modern martial art aikido applies its arm locks in this fashion. Modern day law enforcement personnel are trained in restraining techniques and handcuffing procedures that, for the same reasons, include face-down arm locks to subdue a suspect. No-holds-barred (NHB) contests have shown us that face-down arm locks are rarely successfully applied to an opponent of equal skill. Face-up or face-to-face arms locks are therefore commonplace in the NHB ring. Since weapons are obviously forbidden in NHB, there is no danger of hidden armed counter attacks. If you are much more highly skilled in grappling than your opponent, face-down arm locks are easier to apply and are more prudent. The main reason face-down arm locks or non-face-to-face arm locks are difficult to apply to an opponent of equal skill is that turning your back to your opponent in NHB is the worst position to be in. When your opponent turns his back to you, he has no chance of defending against a barrage of strikes to his body. Therefore, your opponent will be fighting ferociously to avoid turning his back.

The arm lock is especially good when dealing with armed attacks. By controlling the attacker's weapon arm with an arm lock you decrease the likelihood of being injured by that weapon. Aikido, judo, BJJ, and many other martial arts have defensive measures that include the control of the attacker's weapon arm with an arm lock.

Experience in NHB contests has shown that the more effective arm locks are the mostly face-to-face type. Face-down arm locks may be the safe way out but are very difficult to apply on a highly skilled adversary. A combination of judo and BJJ terminology will be used though out this article depending on which terms best fit the situation. Most of the discussion will be from a BJJ perspective, as BJJ's incredible ground grappling arsenal and training put NHB in the spotlight.

The Many Arm Locks

Arm locks that can be highly effective in NHB and other grappling venues include many varieties. The major ones are with the Japanese names: arm breaking cross-hold (*udehishigi-jujigatame*), arm entanglement (*udegarami*), arm hold (*udegatame*), armpit hold (*wakigatame*), stomach hold (*haragatame*), and wrist techniques (*kotewaza*). Most of these arm locks are finished from the ground position, although they may begin from the standing position, like the flying cross-hold (jujigatame) or the armpit hold (wakigatame).

The arm breaking cross-hold is the most common and successful arm lock in NHB contests and judo competition, and there are good reasons for this. First of all, one key point of this lock is that you pinch your legs on the upper body and arm that is being attacked. This gives you excellent control of a thrashing opponent. Secondly, the pressure on the elbow is being applied by your pelvis, the strongest part of the body. These two simple points probably make the arm breaking cross-hold the most powerful arm lock available. Moreover, this arm lock can be performed from a very large number of different positions.

Arm Breaking Cross-Hold

This arm lock can be done from numerous positions. From knee on belly this arm lock is a basic variation, but it is important to know as it is used very often in BJJ.

A-1 Gracie has the side control on his partner and sets-up his hands for the knee on belly position.

A-2 Gracie bounces up to achieve the knee on belly position. From this position, Gracie leans all of his weight onto his knee to pressure his partner.

A-3 Gracie grips the sleeve of his partner's triceps to secure the right arm

A-4 He then swings his left leg over his partner's head and neck.

A-5 To finish the arm lock, Gracie falls to his back while controlling his partner's upper body by pinching his knees together. His partner's thumb must be pointing upward or the elbow won't be locked properly. He lifts his pelvis while holding the attacked arm with both of his hands. This will break his partner's elbow if he doesn't signal his submission.

The arm entanglement is also a very powerful arm lock. In BJJ it goes by many names—Kimura (downward shoulder lock), Americana (upward shoulder lock), and *omo plata* (shoulder lock with the legs) are the most common ones. This lock mostly affects the shoulder joint. It too can be applied from numerous positions. The most common positions when performing this lock are the mount, guard, side control, and half-guard (top and bottom) positions.

Half-Guard Kimura

The Kimura shoulder lock in BJJ is commonly employed from the full-guard and side control, although it is vital to know the variation shown from the half-guard for an effective bottom ground game.

B-1 Gracie is in the half-guard (one leg is trapped in between both of the bottom man's legs). Gracie grips the wrist of his partner's posted left arm.
B-2 Gracie sits up sideways leaning on his right elbow while inserting his left arm over his partner's right elbow.
B-3 Gracie then grips his right wrist with his left hand to create a powerful figure-four lock.
B-4 He falls to his back while keeping his left arm tight to his chest to control the attacked arm.
B-5 To lock the shoulder, Gracie twists his wrists to his partner's ear.

The arm hold is not as commonly used compared with the other two arm locks mentioned previously, although it can be used with the other arm locks in combination attacks when your original move doesn't work. An arm hold can lead into a cross-hold and an arm entanglement can unfold into an arm hold.

The armpit hold is commonly employed from a standing position, but it can be done successfully from ground positions as well. As the name implies, you use your armpit to secure the opponent's elbow. From double arm over hooks when on bottom, modified scarf hold, north-south position or upper four corner hold, and finally when escaping a shoulder hold are just some major ground situations where the armpit hold can be effectively applied. This is one of the most effective face-down arm locks available.

Armpit Hold

This is the basic application of this elbow lock, although it can be used from many ground grappling position as well.

C-1 Renzo Gracie's partner, Andrew Zerling, grips his left collar with right arm. Gracie begins the technique by securing the wrist with both of his hands.

C-2 Gracie then swings his left arm over his partner's elbow while stepping forward with his left leg.

C-3 By using his armpit to secure the elbow and using his hips, Gracie hyper-extends his partner's elbow joint.

The stomach hold is designed almost like a reverse arm breaking cross-hold. As the name suggests, you use your stomach area to hyperextend the elbow. This arm lock is highly effective but is definitely not used as often as arm locks such as the arm breaking cross-hold and the arm entanglement. This powerful technique uses the stomach as the fulcrum. The stomach hold is mostly employed when attacking the turtle or back position.

Wrist techniques are part of BJJ but are down played, as they are not a major joint of the body and may not have fight-ending capability. Even so, the effectiveness of the wrist lock should not be overlooked. Downward and upward wrist locks are the ones used commonly in BJJ. The downward wrist lock can be used to pry free the locked arms of your opponent when finishing jujigatame. The upward wrist lock could be applied when your foe is pushing against you.

Another arm lock that is rarely used in judo, but is applied often in BJJ is the arm crank or bicep cutter lock. This is an arm lock when an arm or leg is inserted in the folded joint and the joint is folded even more to produce a very painful lock. It is mostly done from the guard position. You weave your legs into a triangle around your opponent's arm. You let him pass your guard letting him think he is safe. Once he gets cross side in place, you can lower your knees and lift your pelvis to lock on the bicep cutter. Also if your opponent is defending jujigatame with locked arms you can also use the bicep cutter lock to submit him rather than trying to unlock his arms for an arm breaking cross-hold.

All of these above described arm locks have one major attribute in common. They all require proper mechanics to work correctly. Your body has to be in correct alignment in relation to your opponent's body with the precise force vectors in the right direction. Unless this is correct, you will have to substitute speed and strength for proper mechanics. This may work with lesser opponents, but when faced with bigger, stronger, faster opponents, sloppy technique will get you in trouble. When it comes to arm locks, proper mechanics is the key to proper technique.

Bicep Cutter Lock

D-1 Renzo Gracie is on bottom using his open guard on his partner, Andrew Zerling. Gracie controls his partner with his sleeve grips and a foot on the hip. If his partner was without a jacket, all Gracie would have to do is grip his partner's wrists instead of the sleeves.

D-1

D-2 Gracie weaves his left leg inside his partner's right arm while still controlling the sleeves.

D-3 Then he shoots his right leg along the right side of his partner. This gives his partner the illusion that he is safely passing his guard.

D-4 Gracie triangles his legs and grabs his partner's right triceps from the inside.

D-5 He brings his other hand into play on the triceps. The blade of Gracie's shin is on his partner's bicep muscle. To finish the lock he pulls with his arms, lowers his legs and lifts his pelvis.

Applications

The most popular finishing hold among the Gracie family was the choke; the second most common submission was the arm lock. Leg locks were rarely used to finish a fight by the Gracies. This is probably because their positional grappling kills are so finely honed and hardened that they do not want to lose positional dominance by misapplying a leg lock. If chokes and arm locks are applied with poor technique, there is still a good chance that you will not give up your dominant position. Leg locks can be done in less dominant positions (i.e., inside the guard [in between your opponent's legs]), but most arm locks and chokes require a strongly dominant position (i.e., guard, mount, knee on belly, side control etc…) to be efficacious.

Ideally, the arm lock should be performed from a dominant ground position. Once you have this dominant ground position you have to maintain it while you are trying to apply the arm lock to your opponent. The longer you maintain your dominant position the more fatigued your opponent will become from trying to escape from his poor position. This will increase your chances for a submission. With a dominant ground position you can control the opponent more efficiently with your hips and legs than he can with his own. You can then recruit the whole body into the technique, especially the legs which are one of the strongest parts of your body. High percentages of submissions come from dominant ground positions. It is possible to get a submission from a less dominant position, but it doesn't work as often. Therefore, good positional ground grappling skills are essential for achieving most submissions (Gracie & Danaher, 2003).

The BJJ artist spends countless hours training in passing the guard.* Attempting a leg lock in the guard would be less tempting, especially if the BJJ artist could easily pass the guard and work on the upper body for more effective submissions like arm locks and chokes. Also when performing leg locks your legs are usually open and vulnerable to a leg lock applied on them, which makes performing leg locks risky. Arm locks are much safer moves to go for than your typical leg lock, as when applying arm locks it is next to impossible for your opponent to attempt a submission move of his own. Combinations moves with chokes and arm locks are a staple in the BJJ artist's repertoire. These moves confuse your opponent and therefore help you to force him to submit.

*Note: "Passing the guard" refers to techniques utilized for getting past your opponent's legs to a more advantageous position while your opponent is on the ground in front of you on his back. This passing can be done from a standing or kneeling position.

Passing the guard is a necessary skill if you want do arm locks from the top positions, as performing arm locks while inside a full-guard is next to impossible when grappling with a skilled foe. All your opponent has to do is extend and lift his pelvis or hips to nullify the lock. Now the half-guard (one leg is trapped between your opponent's legs) is a different story. If on top in the half-guard, then an arm entanglement or an arm hold are viable options and can be combined very rapidly with a passing attempt to keep your adversary guessing. Is he trying a submission move or to pass the half-guard? Of course, in the guard, numerous arm locks are available from the bottom. If you are on the bottom in the guard and you repeatedly fail to force your opponent to submit, you can improve your position with a reversal or sweep which will put you in a dominant top position (i.e., mount, side control, knee on belly, not inside the guard). From this dominant top position submissions will be easier to obtain as the opponent has to carry your weight and your movement is less hindered.

As stated earlier, for most arm locks you need a dominant ground position to "control" your opponent. Hence, the title of this chapter, "The Arm Lock: The Technique of Control." Unfortunately, if your foe does not acknowledge defeat by tapping out, he may sustain joint damage from a good arm lock. If properly applied, choking techniques are more humane, as they will only induce temporary unconsciousness.

Conclusion

The arm lock is a versatile and powerful technique for the grappler. It is one of the best methods for dealing with an armed attacker as you gain control of the attacker's weapon arm for disarmament. The arm lock has also proven to be one of the top finishing holds available to the fighters in an NHB contest. The choke tops the list as the ultimate finishing technique, and the leg lock is the least used of the popular submission holds. But for the top Gracie fighters in NHB events, the arm lock is a very close runner-up to the choke. When you are grappling in a tight spot, why not go for an arm lock: the technique of control?

Bibliography

Adams, N. (1989). *Armlocks*. London, UK: Ippon Books.
Gracie, R., & Danaher, J. (2003). *Mastering jujitsu*. Champaign, IL: Human Kinetics.
Gracie, R., Gracie, R., Peligro, K., & Danaher, J. (2001). *Brazilian jiu-jitsu theory and technique*. Montpelier, VT: Invisible Cities Press.
Gracie, R., & Peligro, K. (2003). *Brazilian jiu-jitsu submission grappling techniques*. Montpelier, VT: Invisible Cities Press.
Hoare, S. (1994). *The a–z of judo*. London, UK: Ippon Books Ltd.
Kano, R. (1963). *Kodokan judo a guide to proficiency*. Tokyo: Kodansha.
Shioda, G. (1968). *Dynamic aikido*. Tokyo: Kodansha.
Vazquez, T. (2003). *Defensive tactics for professionals & law enforcement*. www.dtpro.us

The Leg Lock: Technique of Contrasts

by Andrew Zerling, B.S.

Introduction

The leg lock is a finishing or submission hold that attacks any part of the leg from the hip to the toe. The weak part of the leg's anatomy is capitalized on by levering the particular joint beyond its natural range of motion to produce pain and mechanical damage to the attacked soft tissue (e.g., ligaments and tendons) of the leg. Because of the number of injuries sustained as a result of these holds, leg locks have been banned from formal judo contests for some time. Lately however, the leg lock has been brought back into the limelight by the popularity of no-holds-barred (NHB) and jujutsu contests. For the sake of grappling combat effectiveness, many grappling arts have retained leg locks in their systems. Russian sambo and Brazilian jujutsu (BJJ) for instance are grappling arts that have retained leg lock attacks in their system for a broader range of highly effective finishing holds. The powerful and versatile leg lock has many positive and negative aspects associated with it. This article discusses these contrasts.

Positive Aspects

Probably the main reason leg locks have regained popularity in the last decade is that they are very powerful, fight-ending submission holds. With grappling dominating the no-holds-barred contests, it is only natural for the grappler to capitalize fully on his most powerful submission techniques. Continuing a fight with a dislocated ankle is much more difficult than fighting with an injured arm. The legs are your foundation; you need them for mobility. When that is taken away, there is not much you can do. Many examples of the powerful fight ending use of leg locks can be seen in the many no-holds-barred contests held around the globe.

Also another major positive attribute of leg locks is their versatility. Adding leg locks to your grappling arsenal can practically double your finishing holds. Leg locks can be applied from a number of different positions. The most common position is inside the guard (when you are on top and trapped between your opponent's legs). If your attempts to pass the guard repeatedly fail, attacking the legs while inside the guard may be your only real option. Leg locks can even be applied when you are on the bottom mounted, from the mount, cross side, knee on stomach, from the guard on bottom, from the half-guard, and many other positions.

Additionally there is a surprise factor involved with leg locks. Most people are concerned with protecting their neck and arms from submissions. They forget to defend their legs from locks. This is especially true for wrestlers and judo players, since leg locks are illegal techniques in their martial sports. To paraphrase master grappler Gene Lebell: to do something illegal in a fighter's game, something he doesn't know, is the best way to beat any fighter. In numerous no-holds-barred contests you can see the physically more powerful wrestler being swiftly tapped out by the crafty leg lock specialist.

Negative Aspects

Unfortunately there are some negative aspects to leg locks. To quote Gene Lebell: "Leg locks are illegal in judo competition because the leg muscles are so strong that you are unsure of the actual pressure being applied. Thus, your leg could be broken before you decide to submit" (Lebell, 1962: 174). As stated by Alexander Iatskevich, "Leg locks were originally part of judo, of course—and there is still a leg lock in Katame-no-Kata. But leg locks were banned from judo competition early in the 20th century as too many people were being injured. This does not seem to have been the case in sambo, where they are still in use—and where they still win matches. Now, of course, they are illegal in formal judo" (Iatskevich, 2001: 66). To injure one's arm is one thing, but to injure the leg is a more serious, life-crippling occurrence. Twisting leg locks are especially damaging. Some examples of twisting leg locks are heel hooks and toe holds.

Another negative aspect of leg locks is the great possibly of losing positional dominance if you fail to subdue your opponent. If BJJ has taught the martial arts world anything about effective ground grappling, it is that positional dominance is the key to victory. Leg lock attacks can be done from a disadvantaged position, which is a plus. Although the nature of most leg locks is that, if they fail to subdue the opponent, you can be left in an even worse position to grapple from. For example, if you attempt a simple foot lock from inside the guard, your opponent could easily counter you by following your backward motion to mount you. By getting mounted from inside the guard, you have greatly lessened your positional dominance. This drastically differs from most neck and arm grappling attacks. If these finishing holds fail to subdue the opponent, you are usually not going to give up your current position. This gives you the chance to continue attempting submission holds without your position becoming worse.

Basic Leg Lock

Achilles tendon lock from inside the guard.

A-1 Renzo Gracie is inside his partner's guard. Before Gracie goes for any leg lock, he must first break open his partner's legs.

A-2 With a staggered hand grip on his partner's torso, Gracie begins to stand up.

A-3 Gracie unlocks the closed guard with the use of his hips.

A-4 The jujutsu expert opens his partner's guard and traps his partner's left leg with his right arm.

A-5 Gracie wraps his right arm around his partner's left leg while he begins to lower his level.

A-6 Gracie then shoots his left knee tight between his partner's legs. Notice how he controls his partner's hips with his left arm. That keeps his partner from rising up and countering his leg lock.

A-7 Gracie blocks his partner's hip with his right foot. To finalize, he grips his collar with his right arm with the blade of his forearm on the Achilles tendon and arches back with his hips.

Leg Locks in Recent Competition

In 1993 in the first Ultimate Fighting Championship (UFC), The Beginning, when the no-holds-barred (NHB) scene was practically new to North America, there were several good examples of leg lock attack and defense. Ken Shamrock, who was trained in leg locks from the Pancrase circuit, applied a powerful heel hook to a tough striker, Pat Smith, and easily tapped him out. The striker at the time had no idea what was going to happen when Shamrock captured his leg. This illustrated the surprise and efficiency elements.

When Shamrock faced Royce Gracie in the finals of the first UFC, Gracie quickly pulled Shamrock into his guard. Shamrock went for a leg lock on Gracie, but since Gracie was aware of the leg lock dangers and expertly knew the proper counters, Gracie quickly countered the leg lock attempt and attained a dominant top position on Shamrock. From this dominant top position, Gracie easily forced Shamrock to submit. This showed the leg lock positional dominance weaknesses.

When Oleg Taktarov first introduced Russian sambo to the UFC in 1995, he was known for his highly effective leg locks. A large percentage of Taktarov's many victories in NHB have come from his leg locks. Although when up against an expert grappler like Renzo Gracie in Martial Arts Reality Super Fights (MARS) in 1996, Taktarov's apparent leg lock attempt caused him to catch a heel in the face and to be subsequently knocked out. This occurrence illustrated the danger of attacking your opponent's legs, one of the strongest parts of his body.

Today, most NHB fighters are at least somewhat well versed in leg lock attack and defense. This of courses makes the leg lock game now much more complex. Not long ago, during a Yoshida Hidehiko vs. Royce Gracie Pride Shockwave fight in 2002, Yoshida, an Olympic gold medalist in judo, attempted a leg lock on Gracie. Even though Yoshida was not trained in depth in leg lock attacks he attempted one anyway as the fight rules permitted them and the situation presented itself.

In the recent *2002 Combatives Field Manual* for the U.S. Dept. of the Army, three leg locks are shown from ground positions and one from a standing position. The following is stated in the *2002 Combatives Field Manual* (Section 4-7. Leg Attacks): "Leg attacks, although very effective, have the drawback of giving up dominant body position. Therefore, they are not the preferred method of attack. Soldiers must be familiar with them or they will fall easy prey to them. As in all attacks, knowing the technique exists is the primary defense." The earlier *1971 Combatives Field Manual* for the U.S. Dept. of the Army does not present any leg lock information from ground positions, where leg locks are most effective—only a leg lock is shown from a standing position. This is in part because leg locks from the ground positions were not exposed to most in North America in the 1970s. However, they did became popular after being introduced by the Gracie system of jujutsu, which put NHB on the map.

Leg locks, like most submissions, are most potent when done on the ground, as the whole body can be recruited into securing the submission, especially the legs, which are not needed for standing when one is on the ground. Since you are attacking the adversary's leg, one of the strongest parts of his body, most leg locks require that you clamp down on the attacked leg with both of your legs for maximum control and leverage. When one is standing, the legs cannot be used as potently for submissions as when on the ground.

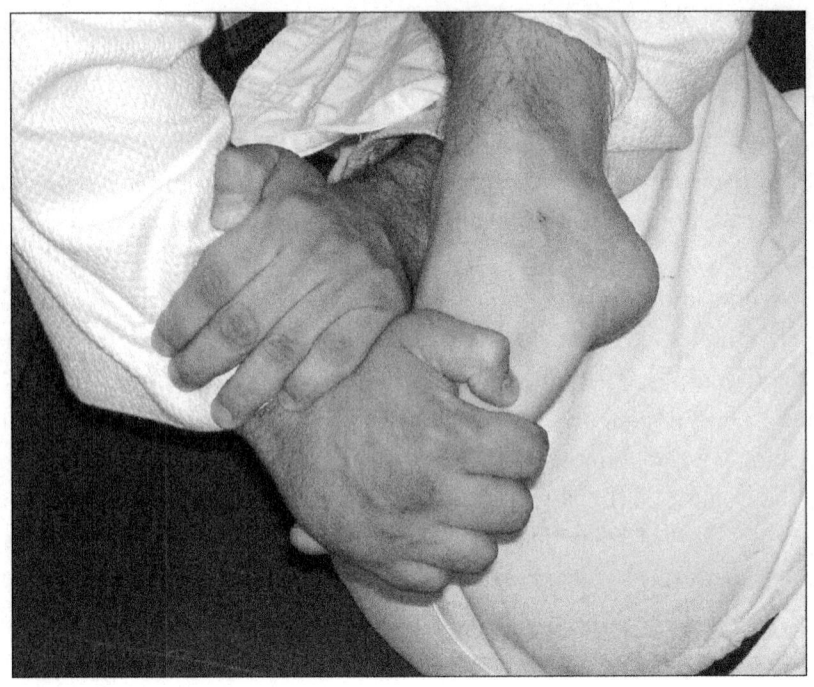

Close-up photo of a toe hold grip.

Martial techniques evolve over time as they become known in competition and fighters adapt. The heat of NHB competition has forged newer and better tools, and the application of leg locks has risen to new heights.

Conclusion

Leg locks have dangerous and negative positional dominance issues associated with them, but they can also be a powerful, versatile, and surprising part of a grappler's arsenal. However, it is still useful to practice the mechanics of the more dangerous leg locks, like the twisting ones, but not utilize them in free sparring where real damage could occur. Although, the twisting leg locks are so brutally effective, they could be used to submit a tenacious opponent if the situation permits.

Additionally, knowing that you could end up in a worse position if you attempt a leg lock could change the strategy of your grappling game. For instance, if you are about to lose the dominant position or are in a less dominant position, attempting a leg lock may be an acceptable gamble. Safety measures can be seen in some jujutsu contests where twisting leg locks are illegal and knee bars are allowed for only the more advanced players. Of course it is important for the advanced grappler to know a variety leg lock attack moves and counter moves for self-defense, as on the street there are no safety rules. Not every technique is perfect. Knowing the pros and cons of a contrasting technique can be the deciding factor of victory.

Bibliography

Gracie, R., & Danaher, J. (2003). *Mastering jujitsu*. Champaign, IL: Human Kinetics.

Gracie, R., Gracie, R., Peligro, K., & Danaher, J. (2001). *Brazilian jiujitsu theory and technique*. Montpelier, VT: Invisible Cities Press.

Headquarters Department of the Army (1971). Combatives, field manual no. 21-150. Washington, DC: Headquarters Department of the Army.

Headquarters Department of the Army (2002). Combatives, field manual no. 3-25-150. Washington, DC: Headquarters Department of the Army. http://www.globalsecurity.org/military/library/policy/army/fm/3-25-150.

Iatskevich, A. (1999). *Russian judo*. London: Ippon Books Ltd.

Lebell, G., & Coughran, L. (1962). *The handbook of judo*. New York: Cornerstone Library.

Vazquez, T. (2003). *Defensive tactics for professionals and law enforcement*. www.dtpro.us.

Core Skills and Four Primary Applications of the Cross-Body Arm Lock

by Steve Scott, B.A.

Author Steve Scott practicing arm locking techniques with Carl Neidholdt. Photograph courtesy of Kevin Minor and used with permission of Kirby Minor. All photographs courtesy of Steve Scott, except where noted.

Introduction

"Coach, this is Shane. I just wanted to call you to thank you." On the other end of the phone was one of my athletes who had moved from Kansas City to Las Vegas for his career about a year before. He's a big, rugged guy who didn't want to stop training in jujutsu and judo, so when he moved, he found a good club to continue his training. Naturally, I asked him why he was calling to thank me. "All that time you had us drill on the spinning jujigatame [cross-body arm lock] really paid off." He went on to explain. "Nobody sees it coming and I've caught a lot of good guys with it. Now I understand why we drilled on it every workout. This move really works!" Shane expressed what many grapplers and martial arts athletes have experienced over the years. The cross-body arm lock (jujigatame) is one of the most versatile and effective techniques in any form of sport or combat grappling.

Jujigatame is an old skill that has stood the test of both time and competition. While the Japanese invented it and made it part of their native jujutsu and judo, it was the Soviets through their grappling sport of sambo that gave jujigatame its distinctive versatility and utilitarian function that has made it so effective and popular.

Historically, the Japanese approach to judo has been to emphasize the throwing techniques, especially in competitive situations. While ground fighting (*newaza*) was used and taught, it wasn't as emphasized as the development of skill in throwing opponents. Then, in the 1960s, the sambo men from the old Soviet Union burst on the international judo stage with their strange approach to gripping, throwing and grappling on the mat. They brought with them a proclivity for the cross-body arm lock. It didn't seem to matter to the sambo men if they threw their opponents or made them submit from an arm lock, they only cared about the end result and that was winning. It wasn't long before the judo world figured out that this particular technique was something worth studying, and studying hard. As a result, numerous top European judo athletes developed exceptional skill in jujigatame. Among them were Neil Adams, Karen Briggs and Steven Gawthorpe from Great Britain, Robert Van Der Walle and Ingrid Berghmanns of Belgium, Peter Seisenbacher of Austria, as well as many others. Of course, the Soviets, and then the athletes from the many former Soviet republics when the communist regime fell, continued to use jujigatame frequently and with effective results.

Today, we see jujigatame used in every form of combat sport, including the mixed martial arts that have become so popular in recent years. Young grapplers, no matter what sport or discipline they practice, can't imagine what it would be like without this workhorse of a technique. Jujigatame is one of the most effective and versatile skills in any grappling activity and this article will focus in on the four core applications that are common to all styles of mat combat. While there are many effective applications and set-ups for jujigatame, if you use the four highlighted in this chapter as the core, primary applications, you will have a thorough understanding of the mechanics of this great arm lock.

Fundamental Skills for All Arm Locks

While this chapter is specifically on jujigatame, I would like to discuss the fact that there are some fundamental, core skills vital to anyone who wants to have a good understanding and ability at arm locks. It's important to study these fundamental skills and not dismiss them, as things only novices should learn. While it's true novices should learn these skills, these are fundamental values that have to be performed every time by anyone of any level of expertise.

Two of the fundamental skills for every successful arm lock are (1) position, and (2) set-ups (there are more, but these two are vital for the other core skills to work). I would like to explain why these two skills are the foundation for further skill development in all arm locks.

We all have heard the old saying in real estate; if you want to sell property, the three most important things are location, location and location. It's the same thing in judo, jujutsu, sambo, and any form of grappling. It could also be easily said for any form of personal combat. If you're not in the right place at the right time, and you don't put your opponent in the wrong place at the wrong time (for him), your arm lock (or any technique) won't work . . . period.

Position is purposely (and with forethought) placing your body is such a way that you can successfully work the move or skill you want to accomplish. An example is, when in groundfighting, get behind your opponent in a wrestler's ride position, controlling at least one of his hips and his near arm. From this initial position, you can sink your legs into his crotch as you climb on his low back and work into the rodeo ride. From this rodeo ride, you have the option to roll him into a sitting position, break him down and flatten him, or work from there to do a hip roll, head roll jujigatame, or other submission hold.

This is what I mean by position. I like to work from the wrestler's ride position, taking the advice of Neil Adams, the World judo champion from Great Britain, when he once told me to "Always get behind your opponent." Conversely, never try to let your opponent get behind you.

A major goal in any groundfighting is to establish a position of control and dominate your opponent. This is especially true when attempting to secure an arm lock. A rule of thumb is to always try to get behind your opponent. Another way of saying this is to try to get your opponent's back. In other words, get behind your opponent, establish a strong position and don't let him see what you are doing. From the other perspective, try never to let your opponent get behind you.

There are many positions that are useful. Fighting off the buttocks (what has come to be known as the "guard" position) is a useful and often effective position. This position is as old as judo itself and it's an instinctive movement for many of us. Remember, in any position you take, have a goal in mind. It may be a really short term goal of simple getting to another, more stable or controlling position. It simply may be to get out of a bad position and get out of trouble. Not every position ends in a cool, sophisticated submission hold with the opponent tapping out. Often being in the wrong position leads to bad results. When you are in a bad position, do what you can to work out of it. An example of a bad position is what I've called the "chicken" position for many years. The chicken position is when an athlete lays flat on the mat, face down with his hands up around his neck and elbows tucked in. We've seen this for years in judo. It's like an ostrich sticking his head in the sand hoping a threat will go away. But that threat never does go away. It simply takes advantage of the situation. When an opponent is in the chicken position, say a silent "thank you" and then work him over. Here is a great opportunity to do just about any breakdown or set-up you want if you are the top person. He's flat on his belly and face and not fighting back and not in a position to be able to fight back.

Another factor to consider about position is that the body has a lot of handles. Every part of the opponent's uniform or clothing is a handle. An opponent's arm is a handle, or a shoulder or hip... just about any part of his body can be used as a handle to pry or lever him into a position where you can gain further control.

Also remember that patience is a virtue in groundfighting. Be methodical and persistent. Go from point A to point B to point C to point D. Remember to take your time, but do it in a hurry!

With all of this in mind, there are specific positions to keep in mind that often lead to a successful set-up of an arm lock. Basically, good groundfighting is establishing a series of positions that lead to a successful submission or hold. Often, an ideal position to get into if you want to secure your arm lock is to get behind your opponent, dig your feet in and aggressively initiate your move. Getting into the ideal position to do an arm lock leads us to the next phase of the core skills, and that is the set-up.

The set-up is the actual breakdown, roll, turnover, entry or application of a particular arm lock. No opponent will lie there and let you stretch his arm, so it's your job to put him in a position so that you can stretch or bend his arm. This chapter's main function is to illustrate as many effective and realistic set-ups for arm locks as possible. The sequence of events that culminate in making an opponent tap out is for a grappler to establish a strong initial position (a ride or guard position, or a follow through from a throw or takedown), followed by further control of the opponent's body by digging the feet in, controlling a wrist or arm and basically using the body's handles to establish more control, followed by the actual set-up, breakdown or roll into an arm lock.

In addition to the concepts of position and set-up, the idea of making a technique work for you is vital to being successful in any form of grappling, whether it be judo, mixed martial arts, jujutsu, sambo, or any form of wrestling. Really, a skillful application of any move or technique is taking a core skill and making it fit you like a glove. Doing it so well, that your ratio of success is excellent, even if your opponents know you're going to do it! Years ago, the great football coach Vince Lombardi said; "Do simple things with consistent excellence rather than complicated things done poorly." Really, it doesn't matter how many arm locks you know, what really matters is that you can do what you know when you need to do it. This leads to the following discussion of the main skills we need to be effective in performing the cross-body arm lock.

The Four Core Skills of Jujigatame

For a good understanding of jujigatame, a number of years ago I developed four basic set-ups or entries into it. By no means did I invent these moves, but I did incorporate them into a disciplined plan of teaching this arm lock. If you learn and practice these four ways to get into the cross-body arm lock and develop good skill at them, you will not only have a thorough understanding and knowledge of the core skills of this arm lock, you will also know four very practical and effective applications and have a thorough understanding of the many groundfighting skills needed to make them work. Not only do you learn the arm lock itself, you learn the practical skills necessary for good groundfighting in general. Really, if you want to excel at this arm lock, it is my belief that a good start is to learn these four core set-ups and review them often. Everyone is different, and different people with different body types will have a preference for one or more of the basic set-ups to the cross-body arm lock.

The four set-ups selected were based on my observation of them and their high ratio of success and adaptability over the years at all levels of competition in a variety of grappling and combat sports. These four entries also teach the value of establishing a good position before attempting to secure the cross-body arm lock. This appreciation for position goes beyond the immediate skill developed in this arm lock, and the subject of position was discussed earlier in this chapter. These four applications can also be used to set up other skills. In some cases, these set-ups may have to be adapted to fit the situation or your own particular needs, but good position is good position and necessary to establish control over a resisting opponent.

The cross-body arm lock is a versatile and effective submission technique and, as I said in the previous paragraph, these four ways to get into it are practical and have proven to be the four most dominant, popular and successful methods of securing this arm lock. If you come away with nothing else from this chapter, I hope you develop good skill in these four basic set-ups for jujigatame.

I like to teach these four set-ups or entries progressively in the following way. Through my years of coaching, it has been my practice to have students do drill training on these four set-ups almost just about every workout. In fact, one of the first skills learned at my club is the back roll cross-body arm lock. If done under proper supervision, arm locks are as safe as any technique, and in fact, safer than many because they can be applied gradually and give your training partner time to submit.

- Back Roll Cross-Body Arm Lock
- Spinning Cross-Body Arm Lock
- Hip Roll Arm Lock
- Head Roll Arm Lock

TECHNICAL SECTION

Application One—Back Roll Jujigatame

The basic entry into the cross-body arm lock is a good follow-through from a throw or takedown. This application is the best way to teach a beginner how to do this arm lock. Learning this entry initially helps teach a beginner how to do many core skills of this arm lock and teaches correct form, which is vital to a high ratio of success.

A-1 This is the starting position. The attacker, Steve, is squatting and may have followed his opponent, Kirt, to the ground after a takedown or throw. Steve has closed the space between the two bodies and begun to establish control with his knees and shins. Steve's right shin is jammed in Kirt's upper back. Steve has already begun to hook under Kirt's arm with both hands and pull it to his chest. Steve is also slightly bent forward and his back is not perfectly straight. This is so he can roll back quickly and apply the arm lock. It's important that Steve be in a squatting position and not on his knees or sitting at this point. If he were on his knees, he would roll Kirt onto his own body.

A-2 Steve has hooked his left foot over Kirt's head. This controls Kirt's head and establishes good control over the entire body as well. Steve has also begun to apply some weight to Kirt's head and his left heel is drawn in tight to add more control to Kirt's head. Steve is actually sitting on Kirt's right shoulder at this point and his knees are beginning to squeeze together. Notice that Steve's weight is centered directly over Kirt's shoulder as he squats over it.

A-3 Steve rolls back onto his buttocks and lower back, making sure to keep his head up and to be constantly looking at his opponent. Steve has maintained tight pressure against Kirt's body as he rolled onto his buttocks. It is important for Steve to not try to put his arm back and catch himself. He should roll back onto his buttocks and lower back and pull Kirt's arm with him as he does. This closes the space between Kirt's near (in this case, right) shoulder and Steve's crotch. Steve's momentum from rolling to his buttocks helps to generate power to pry the arm straight and into proper position to get the most effect from the arm lock. The knees are pinching tightly together, and Kirt is being held tight with Steve's left foot.

A-4 Here is the finish position. Steve has freed Kirt's arm by his back roll and begun to stretch it out and is pinching tightly with his knees for maximum control of his opponent's arm. Notice that Steve is at an angle towards Kirt's head. This is a good finishing position for any type of cross-body arm lock as that extra angle towards the head allows the attacker to put more stress on the shoulder at an angle that makes the bottom man weaker. An example is when you do the bench

press, you have your shoulders square on the bench and you don't lay on the bench with one shoulder higher than the other. The square shoulders give the bottom grappler more stability and strength, so when possible, attempt to angle your cross-body arm lock as shown to make your opponent weaker. Steve is thrusting his hips up as he pulls Kirt's arm straight. This causes pressure on the elbow, shoulder and biceps. Also, from a safety standpoint, please notice that Kirt has his left hand on Steve's leg ready to tap when pressure is applied. All Steve has to do now is pull Kirt's first to his chin and straighten the arm completely.

Application Two: The Spinning Jujigatame

This application is one that you may use often, especially is you prefer fighting out of the guard position on your buttocks or backside. I highly recommend that you practice this entry to the cross-body arm lock every workout performing repetition drills. Doing this set-up teaches more than only the arm lock. It also teaches how to stay round (shrimping) and how to move effectively and quickly on your buttocks and hips when groundfighting. This is an effective set-up for the cross-body arm lock!

B-1 The bottom grappler, Steve, has trapped Kirt's right arm and pulls it into his chest and at the same time, scoots his buttocks in very close to Kirt's knees as shown in the photo. Notice that Steve is almost sitting on Kirt's knees and he is sitting on his buttocks. It's best to not start this while laying flat on your back as you want to stay round and be mobile from this position.

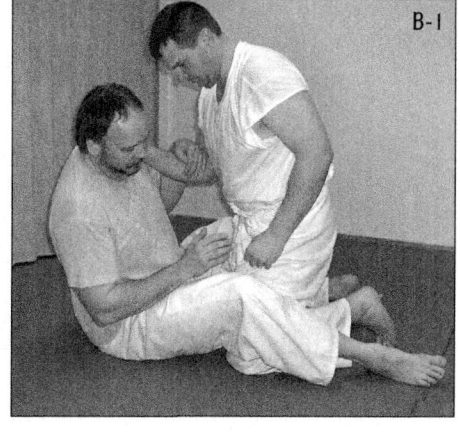

B-2 Again, it's important to start this set-up with the bottom grappler almost sitting on his opponent's knees. If you try to do this from too far away, with too much space between the bodies, the set-up won't work. Steve has curled his body into a tight ball and shrimps to his right side trying to place his right ear as close to Kirt's right knee as possible. At the same time, Steve hooks under Kirt's right knee (with his palm facing him as shown) and draws himself even tighter to Kirt's knee. Steve also positioned his right leg against Kirt's rib cage as shown, making sure to point his toes for extra power. Notice that Steve still has Kirt's right arm tightly trapped to his chest.

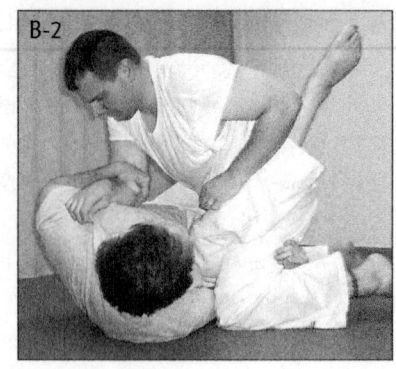

B-3 Steve now hooks his left leg over Kirt's head and neck as shown making sure to point his toes to gain as much hooking power as he can. As he does this, Steve now starts to lift with his right arm that is hooking under Kirt's left leg. Steve drives hard against Kirt's neck and head with his left leg and hard against Kirt's ribs with his right leg. It's important not let your legs "be lazy." In other words, point your toes on both feet and hook hard with the right leg onto your opponent's ribs and side of his body and with your left leg hooked over his neck. Remember, the rounder you are (shrimping to your right side and staying curled up), the more mobile you are and can control your opponent better.

B-4 Steve now has rolled Kirt onto his back and immediately scoots his buttocks in as tightly as possible against Kirt's near shoulder. It is important for Steve to actually roll up onto his buttocks as shown in the photo. By rolling up, the attacking grappler continues in the momentum of the roll and places his hips close to his opponent's near shoulder. As Steve rolls Kirt over, he has controlled Kirt's head with his left leg (in the hooking motion as shown, making sure to keep the toes pointed for maximum power) and has his right leg across Kirt's torso. Steve continues to trap his opponent's arm to his chest in preparation to roll back and apply the arm lock.

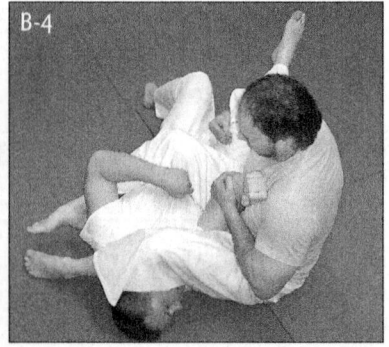

B-5 Steve rolls to his back to secure the cross-body arm lock. To add more power to the lock, Steve will arch his hips as he pulls Kirt's arm to his chin. Also notice that Steve's head is up and off the mat. This gives added leverage to the move and enables the attacking wrestler to see what is going on. Notice that Steve's feet are hooked under Kirt's far shoulder which accordions Kirt's shoulders, making them weaker.

Application Three: The Hip Roll Jujigatame

This application of the cross-body arm lock is very effective and can be used by athletes in all weight classes and by both men and women. It is simplicity in motion and uses the rolling action of your opponent to put him in the right position to lock his arm.

C-1 Bill has gone behind his opponent, Steve, and initiated control with his legs by digging his left leg in Steve's crotch and hip.

C-2 Bill now controls Steve's upper body by hooking his left arm under Steve's left arm and grabbing Steve's left wrist or forearm. The important thing is for the top grappler to control his opponent's entire body, starting with the lower extremities then working to control the upper body.

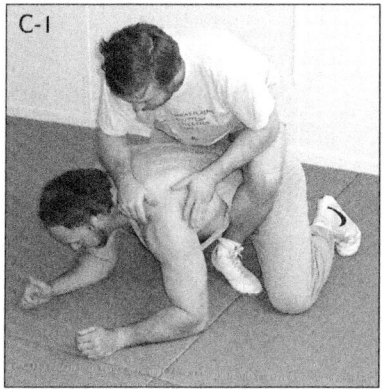

C-3 Bill's body is resting on Steve's back and Bill's body is slightly parallel (as shown in this photo). Bill can either post with this hand or post with his head at this point for stability. In this photo, Bill is showing how you can post your right hand on the mat to stabilize your body as you lay across your opponent. Some athletes prefer to post with the hand and others prefer to post with the head. Also, there's nothing wrong with posting with your hand first, then settling onto the top of your head to stay as round as possible for the upcoming roll.

C-4 If you post on your head, make sure to use the top of your head, and not be facing in one direction or the other. This gives more stability. Bill is posting with his head in this photo and has immediately started to bring his right leg across Steve's body with the intention of hooking it over Steve's head. Bill's right leg will be used to provide the control over Steve's head and provide additional power for the rolling action. When hooking under your opponent's head, jam your foot through. Don't be gentle. You must hook under his head with the foot and leg, making sure to point your toes as shown. Pointing your toes gives your more power in the leg.

C-5 This photo shows how Bill is posting on his head and has started to hook his right leg around Steve's head and neck. Notice that Bill's right foot is pointed, giving it more power as he starts to hook Steve's head. Bill has grabbed Steve's left arm with both of his arms and Bill starts to pull Steve's left elbow to his chest. After establishing these moves, Bill will roll over his left shoulder.

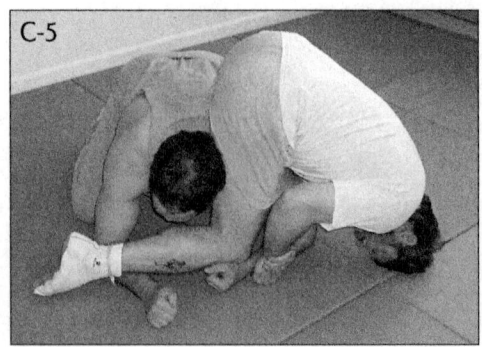

C-6 Bill rolls over his left shoulder and hooks Steve's head as shown in the photo. The reason this set-up is called the "hip roll" is because the attacker rolls in the direction of the bottom man's hip. Bill makes sure to keep his toes pointed giving his right leg more power as he hooks Steve's head. Bill stays round and is in a tight ball as he rolls. He also keeps Steve's left arm trapped firmly to his chest as he rolls. Again, notice that Bill is

tightly in a ball and rolling, forcefully hooking Steve's head with his right leg. Bill's right leg is hooked across his opponent's torso, which further controls the entire body. Bill also keeps Steve's left arm trapped to his chest so when he completes the roll, the arm will be the right place to apply pressure and secure the arm lock.

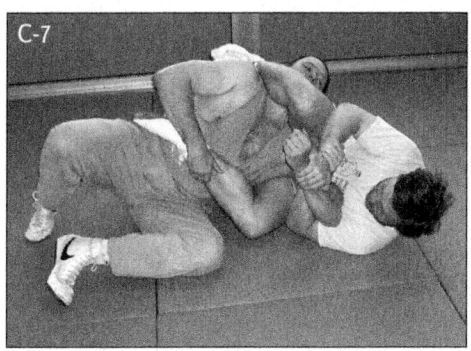

C-7 Bill is midway through his roll and has hooked his right leg forcefully around Steve's neck. Bill's left leg is hooked across Steve's torso and Bill is using both legs to help roll Steve over onto his back. Bill has pulled Steve's left arm tightly to his chest so he can secure the arm lock immediately.

C-8 Bill finishes the roll by coming up onto his buttocks, making sure to keep his hips tight against the near shoulder of his opponent. Bill keeps his right leg hooked firmly over Steve's head and neck. Don't be in a big hurry to flatten out. Get to this position, and then roll back to apply the arm lock. From this leg press position, Bill makes sure to keep his knees squeezed together and hook under his opponent's far shoulder with his feet as shown to insure control. He will then roll back, arching his hips and pulling on Steve's left arm to apply pressure and secure the arm lock.

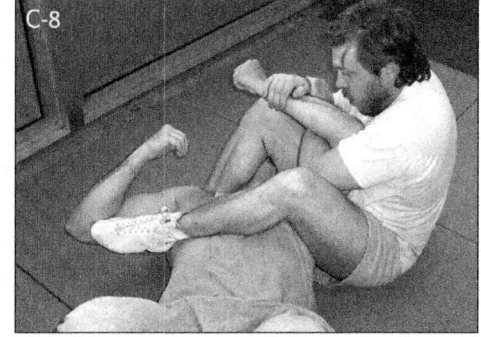

Application Four: The Head Roll Jujigatame

This is a popular application of the cross-body arm lock and seen extensively in judo and sambo competition. I usually don't recommend it for heavyweights as the body weight and girth of the athletes often prevents this from being a viable skill for them. However, try it for yourself and see if it works for you. This really is an effective roll into the cross-body arm lock and is one of the most popular set-ups by the athletes in my own club.

D-1 Bill has got to his opponent's back and digs his left foot into Eric's crotch area. Notice that Bill is coming from Eric's right side and that Bill's left upper leg is across Eric's low back. Bill could have started this wet-up from a rodeo ride as well. Doing it this way gives Bill more momentum than starting from a rodeo ride however.

D-2 Bill hooks his left leg around Eric's left side and the leg is wrapped tightly along the line of Eric's belt, anchoring it. Bill's right leg (on top of Eric's back) is adding a pinching action across Eric's body. Eric's body is controlled by the squeezing action of Bill's legs on his body and Bill's weight is centered over Eric's body at this point. Bill may wish to post with his left arm for stability before posting on his head, or he may choose to roll over Eric's body and immediately post on the top of his head for stability. In this case, Bill as posted with his head and has hooked Eric's near arm (in this case the left) with his right arm. Notice that Bill has placed his left leg at Eric's hip and is in the process of swinging his right leg over Eric's body.

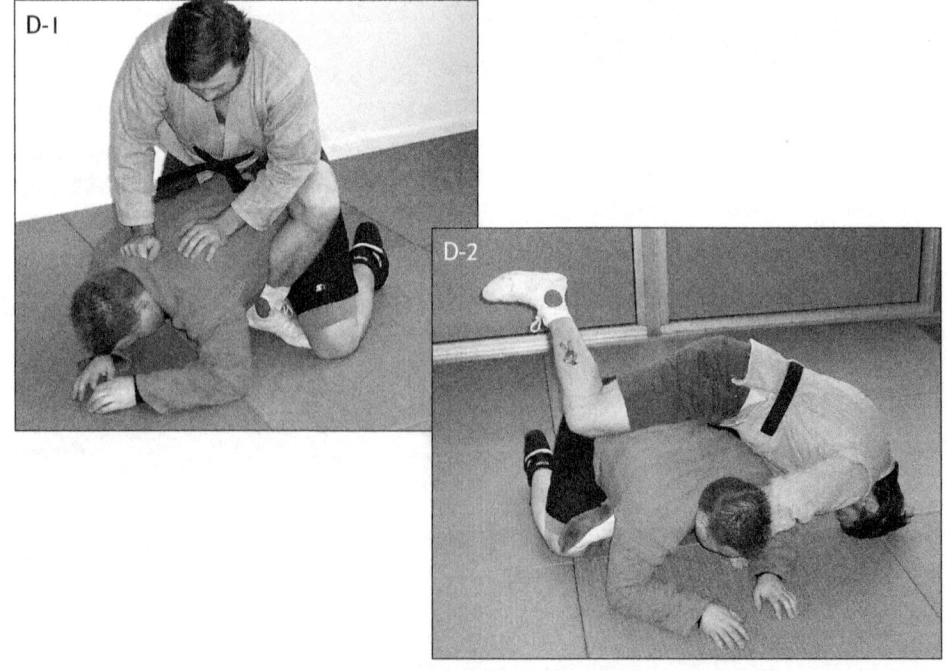

D-3 Bill now has his right leg over Eric's head and neck and (briefly) places his right knee on the mat. Bill places either his shin or the top of his foot on the back of Eric's neck to drive it downward and in. This will help greatly in performing the roll. Bill continues to pull Eric's arm tightly to his chest. An important point here is that Bill's body is round and in a ball and he is rolling over his own right shoulder.

D-4 Bill now rolls onto his right side and pushes Eric's head in with his right foot and shin. As Bill drives Eric's head in tucking it, it forces him to roll over his head. As Bill rolls onto his right side and hip, his own right knee is pointing in the direction of Eric's feet.

D-5 In this photo, Bill has rolled Eric over and has assisted the whole move by hooking Eric's near leg (Eric's left leg) with his left arm. This is called a leg hook or leg drag. If Eric were wearing pants as in judo and jujutsu, Bill could grab the cloth of the pants and use it to drag him over, but the leg hook method is very strong and highly recommended. It is important to mention that this whole sequence of action is explosive and continuous.

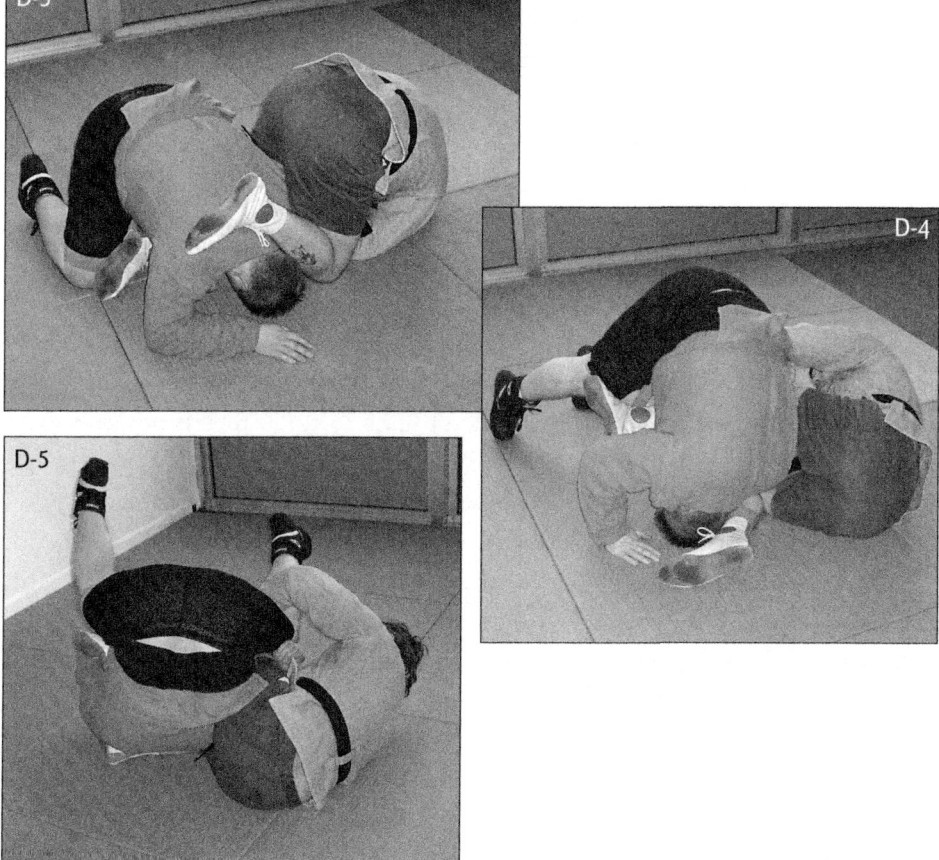

D-6 Bill has rolled Eric over his head and onto his back. Notice that Bill has grabbed Eric's near leg with his left hand at the knee to assist in the rolling action. Bill is now ready to roll back to secure the arm lock.

D-7 Bill finishes the move by rolling back, pulling Eric's hand to his chin and arching his hips. The head roll cross-body arm lock is popular among middle and lightweight athletes and, as said before, used often in competitive situations, especially in judo and sambo.

Making Your Jujigatame Instinctive

As with any skill or technique, if you want to be able to count on doing an arm lock when it counts, whether it's in a competitive situation or in a self-defense encounter, you must make it an instinctive behavior.

The best way to do this is to practice the correct application of the move repeatedly and in a variety of ways. You must drill on the skill you want to master. I recommend that you take your favorite arm lock set-up or application (for instance, the hip roll jujigatame) and do at least 25 to 50 repetitions of it every time you are on the mat. A good way to do this is to do what the Japanese call *uchikomi* or repetition drills. Here's an example of how to do repetition drills: You and your partner decide that you want to do ten sets of three repetitions each. You do three and he does three until you each have performed ten sets. I highly recommend that you offer no resistance to each other during the drill and give each other full cooperation. Remember, the best coach on the mat is often your training partner, so keep moving, but offer advice when your partner is doing something incorrectly. Help each other out. Stay disciplined and work steady, performing the drill until you are done. Don't let the drill end up in a grappling match. There's plenty of time for free practice and going live later. Do each repetition correctly and with efficiency. Don't rush through the drill to get it over.

By doing this, you will get to practice your arm lock for a lot of repetitions, and most important, correctly done repetitions. If you only work on arm locks when you randori or in training matches, you may not get to work on your favorite move much during the course of any workout, if at all. As Shane and I discussed earlier in this chapter, I have my athletes practice the spinning jujigatame every time they train with me. The athletes pair up and I have them alternately perform three spinning jujigatames on each other with 100% cooperation. They do this for about five minutes or so every workout, which gives them the chance to do about 30 or 40 repetitions each. I can't tell enough you how this drill has increased the skill level of the athletes who train with me in a positive way! It's an effective drill that really works.

I recommend you take at least 20 to 30 minutes of every practice to work on a variety of drills to reinforce the skills you already have and improve on new ones. Not only on jujigatame, but every phase of your grappling sport. You can change the level of cooperation in any of the drills, from total cooperation (as described above) to mild resistance, to heavy resistance. You can take any situation that comes up in your sport and turn it into a drill.

The important thing is to be able to perform the skill you want (in this case, jujigatame) without having to think about it. You have to react instinctively to be successful in any sport. If you have to think about how to do something, it is probably too late and the opportunity that was there for you has gone and you may have given your opponent an opening to work his move on you.

The important thing is to be able to perform
the skill you want (in this case, jujigatame)
without having to think about it.
Illustrations by Oscar Ratti.
© Futuro Designs & Publications.

Author Steve Scott practicing
arm locking techniques with Carl Neidholdt.
Photograph courtesy of Kevin Minor
and used with permission of Kirby Minor.

Be Creative

There are many ways to set up an opponent for jujigatame. It's one of those skills that, for anyone who takes the time and effort, can mold it so that it will be an effective part of his personal arsenal. Eventually, you will develop one or more set-ups or breakdowns into this arm lock and make it your own. However, if you study the four core skills outlined in this chapter, you will have a thorough understanding of how and why jujigatame works and how to better make it work for you.

Acknowledgment
I wish to thank Bill West, Carl Neidholdt,
Eric Millsap, and Kirt Yoder for helping
with the photographs for this chapter.

A Study of Armbar Submissions in Ultimate Fighting Championship Contests from 2000 to 2011

by Rhadi Ferguson, Ph.D.

Reilly Bodycomb utilizes an armbar on Stephen Koepfer.
Photography courtesy of the American Sambo Association,
www.ussambo.com

Introduction

The sport of mixed martial arts (MMA) is an extremely challenging form of competitive fighting sport in which the combatants enter a ring or a caged environment wearing only a pair of shorts and compact 4-ounce gloves and fight, with the objective of winning (Cheever, 2009). The sport was projected into the mainstream in 1993 when Rorion Gracie, a Brazilian jujutsu practitioner, and Semaphore Entertainment, a promotional company, introduced the world to no-holds-barred fighting. At that time, MMA had a minimum of safety rules. A combatant could grab an opponent's hair, strike to the groin, head butt, and commit other acts of violence such as eye gouging, all of which are not allowed in today's MMA competitions.

In 2000, New Jersey became the first state in the United States to sanction and regulate MMA, when the New Jersey State Athletic Commission accepted and established the unified rules of MMA, from those originally structured by the Athletic Commission of California (New Jersey State Athletic Control Board, 2002). Although the Athletic Commission of California spearheaded the creation of unified MMA rules, the state of California did not sanction the sport of mixed martial arts until 2005, five years later.

Under the unified MMA rules, the winner is usually the combatant able to do more damage to the other. A combatant can win by various methods: knockout, technical knockout, referee stoppage, submission, or by the judges' decision.

The Armbar Submission Technique

In the first several Ultimate Fighting Championship (UFC) contests viewers watched MMA legend Royce Gracie use a variety of techniques, mainly armbar submissions, to force his opponents to submit or surrender by tapping out. Royce Gracie demonstrated the benefits of submission techniques by winning his first eleven UFC contests by submission. Royce Gracie has since retired with a record of 14-2-1 (wins-draws-losses), and a win-by-submission rate of 85.71% (sherdog.com). One of Royce Gracie's most dominating submission techniques was the arm lock (Zerling, 2005). Thereafter, the armbar submission has become a technical staple in MMA, jujutsu, and grappling arts across the world. On November 17, 2000, in UFC 28, the first UFC event under unified rules, Andre Arlovski defeated Aaron Brink in 55 seconds of the first round with the armbar submission technique, thus achieving the only submission win of the night. The result was a boost in the perceived prominence and dominance of the armbar submission. "An armbar is a kind of joint lock in which the attacker's arm is leveraged and held straight, painfully flexing the elbow joint, and sometimes the shoulder joint. Armbars are a common submission technique used in [jujutsu]" (Ollhoff, 2008: 32). The armbar is a technique utilized by MMA practitioners to get their opponents to submit. Usually the opponent "taps out," signaling surrender or provides a "verbal tap out" by communicating to the referee that he or she acknowledges defeat and would like the contest to end (Zerling, 2005). In some cases, a referee wishing to protect a combatant from injury will execute his prerogative to stop a contest even if a combatant does not submit while trapped in a submission hold. In a study on armbar-caused injuries in MMA, Ngai, Levi, and Hsu (2007) found that upper-limb injuries were the most common injuries in the sport.

Purpose of Research

The techniques of MMA can be categorized as the following: striking and grappling. Striking includes hitting and causing impact to another individual by using one's hands, feet, knees, or elbows. Grappling involves immobilization techniques of trapping, choking, strangulation, takedowns, throws, and pinning (New Jersey State Athletic Control Board, 2002). The goal of a mixed martial artist is to knock out the opponent, force the opponent to tap out, or win the contest by scoring more points than one's opponent.

The spectacular demonstrations of the armbar technique have raised public interest and given rise to exaggerated assumptions of its incidence in the MMA sport and of its importance in training methodology as well. The armbar is thought of as an important technique to finish fights. The popularity of the armbar technique stems from demonstrations in contests, and feeds a public perception of incidence that had not been measured. Therefore, the three objectives of this study are the following: first, to measure and establish the true incidence of armbar submissions per weight class in Ultimate Fighting Championships under a unified set of MMA rules; second, to create a foundation for best practices in competitive UFC, which is currently at its highest level of public interest and popularity in the sport of mixed martial arts; and, third, to use this descriptive research as a forerunner of subsequent articles examining the properties and values of other techniques, as well as training methods in the sport of MMA. The subject contests include all UFC events from UFC 28 of November 17, 2000, to UFC 126 of February 5, 2011.

Methods: Protocol for Collecting Data

The researcher and other qualified associates watched and analyzed every UFC contest from UFC 28 held on November 17, 2000, to UFC 126, held on February 5, 2011, including in-between UFC events, such as UFC Fight Night. The contests were categorized by weight class, and the results noted as to whether they ended with armbar submissions. All data collection was performed by the researcher and the qualified associates who watched the videos in slow motion to ensure validity of the material viewed along with the results.

Presentation of Data and Results

The data collected are summarized and presented as follows: of 1,263 UFC bouts viewed, from UFC 28 to UFC 126, including all UFC shows such as UFC Fight Night, only 51 were found to end in armbar submission. This means that armbar submissions were only prevalent in 4.04% of all the subject contests. All subject bouts were also analyzed per weight division. The weight classes are described and categorized as such in the following table.

Out of 1,263 bouts analyzed, 288 bouts were in the lightweight division, 319 in the welterweight division, 258 in the middleweight division, 217 in the light heavyweight division, and 181 in the heavyweight division. During the subject period, out of the 288 lightweight bouts, 10 were won by armbar submission.

TABLE 1
Weight Class Description

Weight Class	Weight
lightweight	155 lb/70 kg
welterweight	170 lb/77 kg
middleweight	185 lb/84 kg
light heavyweight	205 lb/93 kg
heavyweight	265 lb/120 kg

Out of 319 welterweight bouts, 19 ended via armbar submission. Of 258 middleweight contests, 10 ended via armbar submission. Of 217 light heavyweight bouts, 5 bouts ended via armbar submission. Of 181 heavyweight bouts, 7 ended by way of armbar submission.

Prevalence of the armbar submission by weight class is presented in the following table.

TABLE 2
Armbar Submission Prevalence per Weight Class

Weight Class	Class Description	Number of Matches Analyzed	Number of Matches Ending in an Armbar Submission	Armbar Submission Percentage
lightweight	155 lb/70 kg	288	10	3.47
welterweight	170 lb/77 kg	319	19	5.96
middleweight	185 lb/84 kg	258	10	3.88
light heavyweight	205 lb/93 kg	217	5	2.3
heavyweight	265 lb/120 kg	181	7	3.87

Overall prevalence of the armbar submission is presented in the following table.

TABLE 3
Armbar Submission Prevalence Irrespective of Weight Class

Total Number of Bouts Observed	Total Number of Bouts Ending in Armbar Submission	Total Armbar Submission Percentage
1,263	51	4.04

Armbar submission rates by weight class are compared to the average in Table 4.

TABLE 4
Comparison of Armbar Submission Rates per Weight Class to the Average

Weight Class	Submission Rate
lightweight	3.47
welterweight	5.96
average	4.04
middleweight	3.87
light heavyweight	2.3
heavyweight	3.86

Results

According to the data, the incidence of matches ending in armbar submissions occurred most in the welterweight division (5.96%) and least in light heavyweight division (2.3%). The average percentage of fights ending via armbar submission was 4.04%. The incidence of armbar submission in all of the weight classes, except for the welterweight division, fell below the average.

Conclusions

The armbar appears to have greater prevalence due to the greater number of viewers watching local and lower-tier MMA competitions, where there is much variance among the competitors' technical skill levels. At the lower levels, armbars can be accomplished with less technique and skill, but provide a skewed view of the prevalence of the technique. In this study, the sport of MMA was analyzed at its highest level of proficiency—the Ultimate Fighting Championships (UFC). The data from this highest tier of the sport provides an accurate story concerning the prevalence of the armbar. However, readers must be cautioned to understand that UFC practitioners may have possibly performed the armbar submission technique with lesser skill to get to the top of the sport.

Research for this article started by questioning the percentage of armbar usage as a submission technique. Other questions can be answered through further research, and the practices of MMA can become more evidence based and less belief based. As the sport of MMA grows, professional coaches in the sport will have gained extensive comprehensive skills and know-how to move away from conventional coaching systems towards a more informed and professional scholar-practitioner model, where the coach generates and consumes research simultaneously, ultimately setting standards for the profession at large, and growing the sport as well as its related body of knowledge (Grant, 2003).

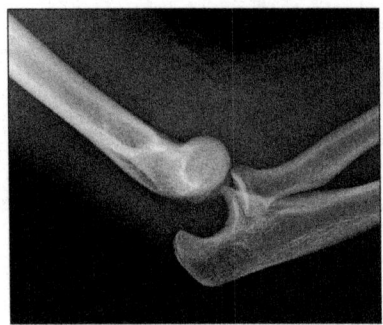

Above: X-ray of dislocated elbow.

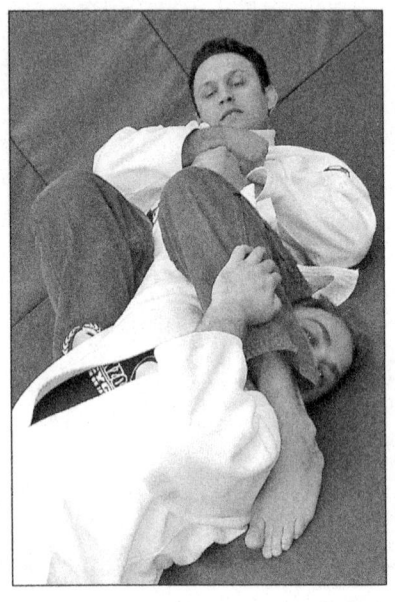

Right: Renzo Gracie demonstrating an arm breaking cross hold (jujigatame) on Andrew Zerling. Photography courtesy of A. Zerling and R. Gracie. See Zerling, 2005.

All high-level MMA athletes will meet the same end sooner or later. No one can compete in a sport at a high level forever; all athletes have a finite period of time in which they can compete at peak level. This means that the chronological real estate of practice is prime territory, and time has to be invested wisely therein. The prevalence of the armbar submission technique may have an impact on how a former elite collegiate wrestler is coached or trained. Due to the fact that the wrestler comes to the sport with less experience in submission holds and more experience in grappling, this research indicates that it may be wiser to spend more time teaching and learning armbar defense than the armbar itself. There have been several UFC champions with few or no submission wins in competition. Researchers in further studies could analyze during which round or which slice of time armbars are more likely or less likely to occur. Addressing the case in point are the following questions: "What is the likelihood of an armbar submission in the last 60 seconds of round 3? The last 90 seconds?" The answers would provide coaches with more data and more scholarly research with which to form a game plan. Such studies would also provide at least some sense of clarity to the longstanding question: "Which is more important: position or submission?" The data would seem to point to "position." Research along similar lines will assist coaching in the sport of MMA to grow and become a more valued profession, such as coaching in other professional sporting domains.

Bibliography

Cheever, N. (2009). The uses and gratifications of viewing mixed martial arts. *Journal of Sports Media*, 4(1), 25–53.

Grant, A. (2003). Keeping up with the cheese! Research as a foundation for professional coaching. Unpublished paper presented at the first International Coach Federation Research Symposium, Denver, Colorado.

New Jersey State Athletic Commission (2011). Available at http://www.state.nj.us/lps/sacb/docs/martial.html

New Jersey State Athletic Control Board (2011). Mixed martial arts unified rules of conduct additional mixed martial arts rules. Available at http://www.state.nj.us/lps/ sacb/docs/martial.html

Ngai, F., Levy, F., & Hsu, E. (2008). Injury trends in sanctioned mixed martial arts competition: A 5-year review from 2002 to 2007. *British Journal of Sports Medicine*, (42), 686–689. doi: 10. 1136/bjsm.2007.044891

Ollhoff, J. (2008). *Grappling: The world of martial arts*. Edina, MN: Abdo Publishing.

Sherdog.com (2011). Royce Gracie submission rates. Retrieved from http://www.sherdog.com/fighter/Royce-Gracie-19

Zerling, A. (2005). The arm lock: The technique of control. *Journal of Asian Martial Arts*, 14(3), 55–63.

A Study of Chokehold Submissions in Ultimate Fighting Championships from 2000 to 2011

by Rhadi Ferguson, Ph.D

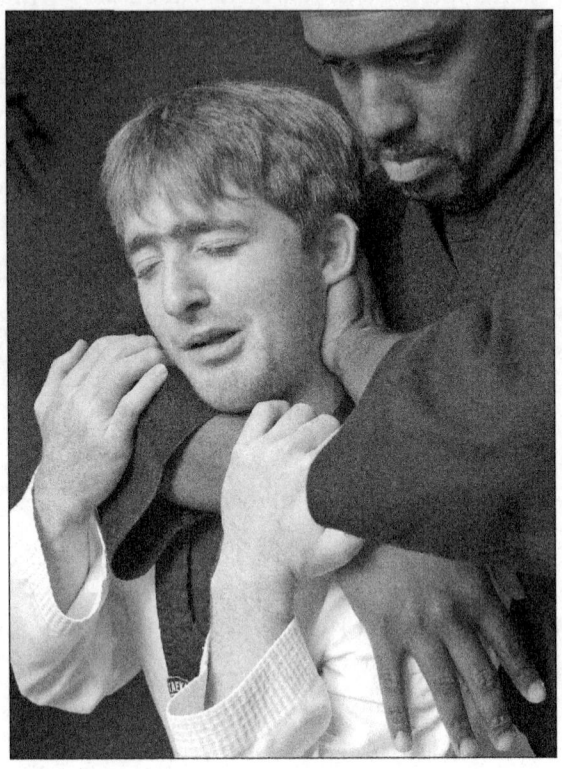

Photograph courtesy of iStockphoto.com

Introduction

The Ultimate Fighting Championship (UFC) is the premier contest organization in the sport of mixed martial arts (MMA), a challenging form of competitive combat in which two combatants enter a ring or caged environment, each wearing only a pair of shorts and compact 4-ounce gloves, and fight with the objective of winning (Cheever, 2009). The only protection each combatant wears is nothing more than a gum shield, a groin guard, and a light smear of petroleum jelly on the eyebrows and cheekbones.

The sport of MMA was projected into the national mainstream in 1993, when a promotional company called Semaphore Entertainment and a Brazilian jujutsu practitioner, Rorion Gracie, introduced the world to the "no-holds-barred" style of fighting (Ferguson, 2011). At that time, MMA only had a few rules, which are still in force today. When MMA entered into the United States of America's mainstream marketplace in 1993, combatants could pull their opponent's hair, strike the groin area, use head butts, and commit other acts of violence, such as fish hooking the mouth, all of which are prohibited in today's MMA competitions (Ferguson, 2011).

Such aforementioned acts of violence are no longer permitted, due to the acceptance of a set of unified MMA rules. In 2000 New Jersey became the first state in the United States to regulate MMA. New Jersey's State Athletic Control Board aided in the construction, acceptance, and establishment of unified MMA rules. Although the state of California actually spearheaded the development of unified MMA rules, it refused to accept and sanction the sport of MMA until 2005, five years after New Jersey did.

Under the unified MMA rules, the winner is usually the combatant who demonstrates more control over the caged environment and his opponent, and who inflicts more damage to the opponent than he receives. A competitor can also win via the following: knockout, technical knockout, referee stoppage, doctor stoppage, submission of the opponent, disqualification of the other opponent, or via judges' decision in the absence of a clear outcome (Wikipedia, 2010).

The Chokehold Submission

Because the thrust of this chapter is to identify the demonstration of a type of submission known as the "chokehold submission," and the fact that the word "choke" has a great deal of ambiguity in the sporting world and in the medical world, for the purposes of this article and its clarity, the term "chokehold" will be utilized to limit any confusion that may result from referring to strangle, strangulation, asphyxiation, choke, smothering, and other such terms. Therefore, all holds that either severely limit or cut off blood supply to the brain or air in respiration will be referred to as a "chokehold." Thus, for the purpose of this chapter, the definition of a chokehold will be to "squeeze or constrict the neck" in order to restrict blood circulation or normal respiration (Oxford Dictionaries, 2011).

The UFC was formed in 1993. In the UFC 1 contest on November 12, 1993, viewers watched MMA legend and pioneer Royce Gracie of Brazil utilize various chokeholds to force his opponents to submit via tap out. Royce Gracie demonstrated the strength and benefits of being proficient with chokeholds by using them to defeat two of his three opponents in UFC 1 (Sherdog.com, 2011). Since then, the chokehold has become a staple technique in MMA. On December 16, 2000, in UFC 29, the second UFC event held in Tokyo, Japan, under the unified international set of MMA rules, Pat Miletich defeated Kenichi Yamamoto at 1 minute and 57 seconds of the second round with a chokehold, thus achieving the first chokehold submission win in UFC history (UFC.com, 2011). The chokehold, like the armbar or the leglock, is the name of a group of techniques utilized by MMA practitioners to force their opponents to tap out or submit. Usually, individuals being choked tap out to signal their surrender due to their inability to vocalize their surrender. In some cases, a combatant may choose to fight the choke and try to use every ounce of power to break out from the hold, which usually leads to the combatant losing consciousness. At this juncture, referees must impose their professional prerogatives and rights to stop the action and award the bout to the winner by reason of his dominant technique.

Purpose of Research

The purpose of this study is to provide mixed martial arts professionals with information to assist and guide their training practices for victorious outcomes. Eleven years of Ultimate Fighting Championships and literature were reviewed in order to determine the prevalence of the chokehold submission.

The techniques of the sport of MMA can be split into two main categories: striking and grappling. Striking includes hitting the opponent with a limb, such as punching, elbowing, slapping, kicking, kneeing, or stomping. Grappling includes immobilization techniques, such as chokeholds, strangleholds, holddowns, pins, takedowns, and throws (New Jersey State Athletic Control Board, 2002). The goal of each combatant in an MMA sporting contest is to win. The methods by which that can be accomplished are by knockout, tap out, or by scoring more points than the opponent.

Since the beginning of the UFC, the chokehold has been a prominent technique utilized in securing victory. Although simple and effective, it is often overlooked and categorized as a basic technique. Therefore, the purpose of this study is threefold: first, to measure and establish the true incidence of the chokehold submission technique per weight class in the UFC under a unified set of MMA rules; second, to create a foundation for best practices for competitors and coaches in the UFC; and third, to use this descriptive research in conjunction with subsequent articles to examine the properties and values of other techniques as well as training methods in the sport of MMA. The subject contests that were reviewed included all UFC events from UFC 28 of November 17, 2000, to UFC 126 of February 5, 2011.

METHODS

Protocol for Collecting Data

The researcher and other qualified associates watched and analyzed every

UFC contest, from UFC 28, held on November 17, 2000, to UFC 126, held on February 5, 2011, including in-between UFC events, such as UFC Fight Night. The contests were categorized by weight class, and the results noted as to whether they ended with chokehold submissions. All data collection was performed by the researcher and the qualified associates who watched the videos in slow motion to ensure validity of the material viewed along with the results.

Presentation of Data and Results

The data collected are summarized and presented as follows: of 1,263 UFC bouts viewed from UFC 28 to UFC 126, including all UFC shows such as UFC Fight Night, 226 were found to end in chokehold submission. Choke submissions were found to be prevalent in 17.89% of all the subject contests. All subject bouts were also analyzed per weight division. The weight classes are described and categorized as such, shown in Table 1 below.

TABLE I

Weight Class Description in Ultimate Fighting Championship Events

Weight Class	Weight
lightweight	155 lb/70 kg
welterweight	170 lb/77 kg
middleweight	185 lb/84 kg
light heavyweight	205 lb/93 kg
heavyweight	265 lb/120 kg

Out of 1,263 UFC bouts analyzed, 288 bouts were in the lightweight division, 319 in the welterweight division, 258 in the middleweight division, 217 in the light heavyweight division, and 181 in the heavyweight division. During the subject period, out of the 288 lightweight bouts, 73 were won by chokehold submission. Out of 319 welterweight bouts, 53 ended via chokehold submission. Of 258 middleweight contests, 61 ended via chokehold submission. Of 217 light heavyweight bouts, 26 bouts ended via chokehold submission. Of 181 heavyweight bouts, 13 ended by way of chokehold submission.

Prevalence of the chokehold submission by weight class is presented in the following table.

TABLE 2
Chokehold Submission Prevalence per Weight Class

Weight Class	Class Description	Number of Matches Analyzed	Number of Matches Ending in an Chokehold Submission	Chokehold Submission Percentage
lightweight	155 lb / 70 kg	288	73	25.34
welterweight	170 lb / 77 kg	319	53	16.61
middleweight	185 lb / 84 kg	258	61	23.64
light heavyweight	205 lb / 93 kg	217	26	11.98
heavyweight	265 lb / 120 kg	181	13	7.18

Renzo Gracie works on the mat with Andrew Zerling.
Photograph courtesy of
A. Zerling and R. Gracie.

Overall prevalence of the chokehold submission is presented in the following table.

TABLE 3
Chokehold Submission Prevalence
Irrespective of Weight Class

Total Number of Bouts Observed	Total Number of Bouts Ending in Chokehold Submission	Total Chokehold Submission Percentage
1,263	226	17.89

Chokehold submission rates by weight class are compared to the overall average in the following table.

TABLE 4
Comparison of Chokehold Submission Rates per Weight Class to the Average

Weight Class	Submission Rate
lightweight	25.34
welterweight	23.64
average	17.89
middleweight	16.61
light heavyweight	11.98
heavyweight	7.18

Right: Renzo Gracie with Andrew Zerling illustrating a guard front triangle choke.

Photograph courtesy of A. Zerling and R. Gracie.

Results

According to the data, the incidence of matches ending in chokehold submissions occurred most in the lightweight division (25.34%) and least in the heavyweight division (7.18%). The average percentage of UFC fights in all weight classes ending via chokehold submission was 17.89%. The incidence of chokehold submissions for the welterweight, light heavyweight, and heavyweight divisions fell below the average.

Conclusions

As the UFC and the sport of MMA grow, professional trainers and coaches will gain extensive comprehensive skills and knowhow, and will tend to move away from conventional coaching systems toward a more informed and professional scholar-practitioner model, whereby the coach generates and consumes research simultaneously, ultimately setting standards for the profession at large, and growing the sport as well as its related body of knowledge (Grant, 2003).

This type of research enables researchers and professionals to build a foundation for the sport that spurs the creation of practices, fight camps, curricula, and schedules based upon research, data, and validated curriculum outcomes. In the MMA coaching profession, many coaches guess and many fighters "hope" that the well-informed professional coach will make sound, calculated, and scientific decisions that limit chance and randomness as much as possible.

In terms of training, fighters often abandon tried and true basic techniques for flashier and more appealing ones. The data herein suggest that, having a basic understanding of chokeholds, how to apply them, and how to defend against them is of utmost importance to coaches and combatants. In a former research article, the author reported that the average incidence of the armbar submission in the UFC from 2000 to 2011 was 4.04% (Ferguson, 2011). The incidence of the armbar submission in UFC matches pales in comparison to the average prevalence of the chokehold submission, which is 17.89%. The comparison indicates that coaches should spend the majority of their time teaching their MMA competitors the techniques of administering and defending against chokeholds, rather than armbars. Specific information such as this allows coaches to design a curriculum that is chronologically sound in terms of their investment of time in teaching of attack and defense techniques, ring craft, physical training, and selfmanagement.

In this study, the sport of MMA was analyzed at its highest level—the Ultimate Fighting Championship (UFC). The data from this level of the sport provides an accurate story concerning the prevalence of the chokehold submission.

All high-level MMA athletes will demonstrate their talents, growth and acquisition of skills, achieve their peak performance levels, and realize a decline in performance sooner or later. No one can compete in a sport at a high level forever; all athletes have an endpoint to their peak capability, a time when they will no longer be able to compete at a high level. This means that during the developmental years and time during, before, and slightly after their peak, there is a piece of chronological real estate of practice that is prime territory and, therefore, time is of the essence. The prevalence of the chokehold submission technique may have an impact on how a former elite collegiate wrestler is coached or trained. Due to the fact that the wrestler comes to the sport with less experience in submission holds and more experience in grappling, this research indicates that it may be wiser to spend more time teaching and learning choke offense and choke defense than the armbars. There have been several UFC champions with few or no submission wins in competition. Researchers in further studies could analyze during which round or which part of the time frame of a bout a chokehold is more likely or less likely to occur. Addressing the case in point are the following questions: "What is the likelihood of a chokehold submission in the last sixty seconds of round 3? Or, in the last ninety seconds?" The answers would provide coaches with more data and more scholarly research with which to form a game plan based on their combatant's and the opponent's historical performances, demonstration of energy, and their displays of levels of effectiveness during phases of the bout. Research along similar lines will assist coaching to grow and become a more valued profession in the sport of MMA, and equal the status of coaching in other popular sporting domains.

Bibliography

Cheever, N. (2009). The uses and gratifications of viewing mixed martial arts. *Journal of Sports Media*, 4(1), 25–53.

Ferguson, R. (2011). A study of armbar submissions in ultimate fighting championship contests from 2000 to 2011. *Journal of Asian Martial Arts*, 20(2), 74–81.

Grant, A. (2003). Keeping up with the cheese! Research as a foundation for professional coaching. Unpublished paper presented at the first International Coach Federation Research Symposium, Denver, Colorado.

New Jersey State Athletic Control Board (2011). Mixed martial arts unified rules of conduct. Available at http://www.nj.gov/lps/sacb/docs/martial.html

Oxford Dictionaries (2011). Available at http://oxforddictionaries.com/definition/strangle

Sherdog.com (2011). Royce Gracie submission rates. Retrieved from http://www.sherdog.com/fighter/Royce-Gracie-19

UFC.com (2011). Available at http://www.ufc.com/fighter/Pat-Miletich

Wikipedia (2010, September 4). Mixed martial arts rules. Available at http://en.wikipedia.org/wiki/Mixed_ma

index

achilles tendon lock, 11, 30–31, 59, 60–61
Adams, Neil, 12, 69, 71
age of competitors, 2, 5–6
aikido, 47–48
Almeida, Ricardo, 10
American/Americana lock, 9, 24, 50
anaconda choke, 28
Anderson, Lowell, 5
Andre, Jermaine, 14
Arlovski, Andre, 86
armbar, 1, 8–9, 13, 15–16, 23, 25, 28–31, 85–91, 94, 98-99
arm triangle choke, 9, 23, 28, 30–31
arm breaking cross-hold, 48–49, 53, 90
arm lock, 9, 11, 23, 36, 43, 47–56, 61, 68–84, 86
armpit hold, 48, 52
back roll cross-body armlock, 73–75
Belfort, Vitor, 6
Berghmanns, Ingrid, 69
bicep cutter lock, 53–54
Brazilian jujutsu/jiu-jitsu, 2, 8–9, 16, 20, 23–24, 27–28, 31–32, 35–36, 41, 47, 57, 61, 85, 92
Briggs, Karen, 69
Brink, Aaron, 86
Bustamante, Murilo, 8
carotid artery, 17, 36–37, 41–42
Carter, Shonie, 3
Coleman, Mark, 22, 24
Cook, Bob, 1, 13
Couture, Randy, 24–26
cross-body arm lock, 68–84
Desouza, Tony, 5
entanglement, 48, 50, 52–53, 56
Fedor, Emelianenko, 32
Freeman, Ian, 12
front shoulder choke, 39–40
Gawthorpe, Steven, 69
Ghosen, Tiki, 1, 13
gi, 28, 37–45
Gibson, Lance, 14
Gilstrap, Bob, 13, 16
Gracie, Helio, 27

Gracie, Renzo, 35–67, 90, 96-97
Gracie, Rickson, 27–28, 30, 37
Gracie, Rorion, 85, 92
Gracie, Royce, 4, 6, 19, 27–28, 37, 42–43, 65–68, 86, 93
Greco-Roman wrestling, 16, 20, 22, 24
groin strikes, 3, 38, 85, 92–93
ground and pound, 22–27, 31-32
guard, 8–9, 11, 16, 22–23, 37, 39, 42–43, 50-59, 61, 63–65, 71-72, 75, 92
guard front triangle, 42–43
guillotine choke, 5, 7, 9, 12, 23, 30, 37
hair pulling, 3, 85, 93
half-guard, 22, 50-51, 55-58
half-guard Kimura, 51
head roll, 71, 73, 80, 82
height of competitors, 5–6
Hidehiko, Yoshida, 21, 65
hip roll, 71, 73, 77–79, 82
Jackson, Eugene, 10, 12
Jackson, Quinton, 21
joint lock, 6, 14, 22, 47, 86
judo, 9, 16, 20–21, 23–24, 36–38, 40–43, 45, 47–49, 53, 57–58, 65, 68–72, 80–82
jujigatame, see armbar.
Kerr, Mark, 24–25
key-lock, 10, 14-15
Kimura, 10, 14, 24, 28, 30–31, 47, 50
knee bar, 11, 23, 67
knee lock, 64
knee strikes, 3, 11, 20
Kosaka, Tsuyoshi, 15
leg lock, 11, 23, 31, 43, 55–67
leg lock escape, 63
Light, Zach, 9
mata leão (lion killer choke), 35
match length, 3–4
Mello, Marcello, 5
Miletich, Pat, 93
Mir, Frank, 11
Moore, Hommer, 15
mounted cross choke, 37–38
Muay Thai, 17
neck crank, 9, 22, 24–25, 28, 30–31

Neidholdt, Carl, 68, 84
Newton, Carlos, 10, 13, 16, 19, 27–29
no-holds-barred, 1, 48, 57–58, 65, 85, 92
Nogueria, Antonio Rodrigo, 27
omo plata, 50
Ortiz, Tito, 7, 21, 24–26
Pancrase, 2, 11, 30, 65
passing the guard, 55
Pedro, Jimmy, 45
Penn, B.J., 32
Randleman, Kevin, 17
rear gi choke, 40-42
rear naked choke, 7, 13, 23, 24, 28, 30–31, 35
Remedios, Liegh, 7
Roberts, David, 6
Rockel, Keith, 12
Rodriguez, Paul, 5
rules, 1–4, 32, 36, 40, 65–67, 85–87, 92–94
Rutten, Bas, 19, 30–32
Sakuraba, Kazushi, 30
Sakurai, Hayato, 32
Salaverry, Ivan, 8
sambo, 16, 20, 23, 32, 57–58, 61, 65, 69–70, 72, 80, 82, 85
sankakujime, see triangle choke.
Sato, Rumina, 23, 30
Seisenbacher, Peter, 69
Semenov, Andrei, 8
Serra, Matt, 3
Shamrock, Frank, 4, 7, 11, 14, 21, 65
shuaijiao, 21
side control, 37, 39, 44, 49–51, 55–56
side control sleeve choke, 44
Sobrol, Reanto, 17
spinning cross-body armlock, 69, 73, 75–77, 83
Spratt, Pete, 9–10
striking, 3, 6–7, 11, 14, 16–17, 20–24, 26, 29–32, 36–37, 41, 45, 48, 65, 86–87, 94
strangulation, 35–36, 40, 45, 87, 93
submission, 2–3, 5–9, 11–12, 14, 16–17, 20, 22–28, 31–32, 37–39, 41, 43, 47, 50, 55–58, 61, 66, 71–73, 85–86, 91–99
submission wrestling, 16, 20, 23
Sudo, Genki, 7, 19, 30–32
takedown, 16, 20–22, 37, 43, 72–74, 87, 94
Taktarov, Oleg, 65
Tanner, Evan, 15
toe hold, 23, 30–31, 58, 61–62, 66
triangle choke, 8–10, 17, 23, 25, 28–31, 42–43
shimewaza, see strangulation.
udegarami, see entanglement.
Van Clief, Ron, 6
Van Der Walle, Robert, 69
weight classes, 4–6, 14, 24, 27, 30, 32, 77, 87, 89, 95, 97
Western freestyle, 16, 20, 22, 24
Williams, Pete, 11, 15
Yamamoto, Kenichi, 93
Yarbrough, Emmanuel, 5
Zinoviev, Igor, 14

Printed in Great Britain
by Amazon